AFTER WINTER COMES SPRING

How To Find Joy In The Journey From Deep Despair

KATHY TOMLINSON

Scripture quotations marked (NLT) are taken from the New Living Translation, copyright © 1996, 2004, and 2015 by Tyndale House Foundation. Used by permission of Tyndale House Publisher, Inc. Carol Streams, Illinois 60188. All rights reserved.

Scripture taken from the Holy Bible, New International Version®, NIV®. Copyright © 1973, 1978, 1984, 2011 by Biblica, Inc.™ Used by permission of Zondervan.

Scripture quotations marked (TPT) are from The Passion Translation, copyright © 2017, 2018, 2020 by Passion & Fire Ministries, Inc. Used by permission. All rights reserved. ThePassionTranslation.com

Scripture quotations taken from the Amplified® Bible (AMP), Copyright © 2015 by The Lockman Foundation. Used by permission. lockman.org

Scripture quotations are from The ESV Bible (The Holy Bible, English Standard Version) © 2001 by Crossway, a publishing ministry of Good News Publishers. Used by permission. All rights reserved.

ISBN: 979-8-9994802-0-0 (Paperback)
ISBN: 979-8-9994802-1-7 (e-book)

Interior book design: Courtney Creative Designs
Editorial services: Nzadi Amistad Editing and Writing Services
Photograph Services: Amber Gallimore Photography

For more information: visit kathytomlinson.com

AFTER WINTER COMES SPRING

All glory for this book belongs to God. I pray you see my heart in the struggles and tension I've experienced. Through it all God has been faithful and patient. He called me to write this book for those who have lived in shame, lived without knowing forgiveness. He is the Great Healer. He wants a relationship with you. Jump on that Jesus Journey. It's a ride for a lifetime!

TABLE OF CONTENTS

INTRODUCTION

Part of being a human being is being able to make choices. Because of some of the choices I made, I've spent many years of my life being hard on myself. I know I am not the only one who has made a choice or several choices that I deeply regret, and that regret has caused me to live in my own personal hell. I have found that the only way to overcome the choices I've made is to hand them over to God.

And of course, this is a lot easier said than done. I have had amazing advancements and devastating setbacks along this road.

And what a journey this has been. Years ago, I was mired in choices I wish I had never made. Yet, as I continued walking my path, I found redemption through Jesus. As a result, I heard God and Jesus calling to me, to share my heart, to share who He has become to me. This is the story of how that started…

Me: Are you kidding me, God?
God: No, it will be ok.

Me: I don't want to.

God: Why?

Me: What will people think? They're going to hate me, judge me, criticize me.

God: No, they won't.

Me: Have you looked at people lately?

God: I have. I created them. Be strong and courageous. Besides, I am with you.

Me: I still don't want to. It means I have to look back at where I've come from. It's painful. I don't like looking at myself that closely.

God: I'll be with you. I will strengthen you. I have prepared you for this.

Me: But I'm not a writer. I don't know what to say or how to say it.

God: I'll give you the words.

Me: I still don't know about this.

God: Go read My book.

Me: (The names of Old and New Testament people start streaming through my mind: Abraham, Joseph, Elijah, Elisha, David, Jeremiah, Isaiah, Joshua, Hosea, Daniel, John the Baptist, Jesus, Peter, Saul (later Paul), James, Timothy. I pause on Moses).

Moses, what an interesting time to be born, eh? If you're unfamiliar with his story, that's ok. You can read it all in the book of Exodus in the Bible. Or, if you prefer, here's a little background: there had been a famine throughout the land (Israel, Egypt, and that area of the Middle East), and the Hebrew people had settled as a relatively small group in Egypt.

At first, they were welcomed there with open arms. But as time went on (let's be real, it was centuries), they became prolific and multiplied (into hundreds of thousands of people from about seventy to begin with). The leadership in Egypt had changed, and the new Pharaoh was fearful of the number of people there were. The Hebrews were seen more as a threat and needed to be oppressed and taken into bondage. So, the Egyptians enslaved the Israelites and conscripted them to build cities for the Egyptians. The harsher they were treated, the more the Israelites multiplied and grew. This scared the Egyptians, so they (the Egyptians) "made their lives bitter with hard bondage—in mortar, in brick, and in all manner of service in the field. All their service in which they made them serve, was with rigor" (Exodus 1:14, New King James Version [NKJV]).

Because they feared the Hebrews so much, the king of Egypt told the midwives to kill all the male children. But the midwives feared God and told the king the Hebrews delivered too quickly.

Hence, the birth of Moses. He had been hidden in the bushes; the Pharoah's daughter saw him and had a Hebrew slave bring him to her. So, he ended up being a Hebrew raised in Egyptian royalty.

One day, Moses saw an Egyptian beating a Hebrew slave, and because he thought no one would see, Moses killed him. But a Hebrew did see it and called him out on it the next day. Moses fled in order to not get caught. He ended up in another land called Midian, where he helped a man named Jethro. Now, Jethro only had daughters, and they struggled to feed and water their flocks because the other shepherds around them would drive them away. Jethro was grateful Moses had helped his daughters and, in response, gave Moses one of his daughters in marriage. Moses was content to stay and live for a time there.

Eventually, that pharaoh died, and other, more horrible pharoahs came into power, and the people of Israel groaned and cried out due to their bondage. God heard and acknowledged them. Now, it was time to help the people. They had been there for about 400 or so years.

God chose Moses to use His voice. God presented Himself to Moses as a burning bush, and when Moses went near, he realized it was God, who told him He saw the oppression of the people and wanted to deliver them to a land flowing with milk and honey, the land God had promised to them centuries earlier through Abraham. This is Exodus 3, and here is where my thoughts of Moses come to light. God told Moses that He was sending him to bring His people out of Egypt. Moses was kind of like, "What? I'm nobody. What are you talking about?" (MY take on how Moses felt!) God tells him that He will be with him. Moses comes up with an excuse, "Well, when I get there, I don't know who I'm supposed to tell them sent me." (Again, my take!)

Now, every version I've looked at uses all capital letters when God tells him who to say sent him: "I AM WHO I AM" (Exodus 3:14, New International Version [NIV]). Say I AM sent you. I like to think that is all I need to hear. But as you can gather from the conversation at the beginning, I'm much more like Moses, in that he continued to argue, too. (Insert head slap emoji!) That was only the beginning of that section, because it takes God through verse 22 to try to get Moses to understand. He doesn't.

Moses gives God another reason not to use him, and God responds with signs and wonders, not once, not twice, but a third time. But did Moses listen? Nope. "I can't speak right," he says. Oops. God still doesn't take no for an answer.

Then Moses says, "Please ask someone else." That angered God, so He had Moses's brother Aaron (who was still in Egypt) come from Egypt to be the one to go back with Moses to verbalize out loud the words given to Moses by God.

They did this together, and after changing water into blood, bringing frogs, lice, and flies, causing livestock to be diseased, bringing boils, hail, locusts, darkness, and finally death, Pharaoh finally relented and let the people leave with Moses.

It's quite an exciting book in the Bible. Exodus is the second full book of the Bible. It's got forty chapters, and I do recommend reading it because I've just given an overview simply to show that while I've argued a bit with God about writing this book, I'm not alone. There have been others along the way that have their reasons for not

doing what God is calling them to do. The Bible is full
of stories of people hesitating. I'm not saying that is ok,
but I am saying that working through it all with Him is a
good thing.

Some stories haven't ended well. Even Moses
really didn't end well. But you'll have to read Exodus
to find out Moses's ending. And while I've argued with
God and questioned Him throughout this entire process,
He's been faithful to me. Encouraging me along the way.
Sometimes with His Word, sometimes using others to
speak to me.

"Even when I walk through the darkest valley,
I will not be afraid, for you are close beside me.
Your rod and your staff protect and comfort me.
You prepare a feast for me in the presence of my
enemies. You honor me by anointing my head
with oil. My cup overflows with blessings."

Psalms 23:4-5,
New Living Translation (NLT)

This is my journey, written for people who long
for forgiveness for past mistakes. For people who long
to be free of self-condemnation and self-hatred. Free

from fearing what people will think. Free to realize that mistakes are a (sometimes) wretched part of life, but God will redeem those mistakes. He will use those mistakes to bring to others the knowledge and acceptance of redemption, forgiveness, and life. Even when those mistakes are of your own choosing, there is life in Jesus, there is hope, and there is love.

> "By living in God, love has been brought to its full expression in us so that we may fearlessly face the day of judgment, because all that Jesus now is, so are we in this world. Love never brings fear, for fear is always related to punishment. But love's perfection drives the fear of punishment far from our hearts. Whoever walks constantly afraid of punishment has not reached love's perfection."

> 1 John 4:17-18,
> The Passion Translation (TPT)

Some who read this journey will not understand it. Some will despise, hate, and disagree. But God is calling me to share my journey with those who need to hear it, with those .who have had similar experiences and crave the joy of knowing redemption. He will bring you from your place of pain to your place to reign. You can be forgiven by God, by your unborn children, by your family. You can forgive yourself.

"A person may have many ideas concerning God's plan for his life, but only the designs of God's purpose will succeed in the end."

Proverbs 19:21, TPT

THE
BEGINNING

When we were young, did we really know or understand how the choices and decisions we made would impact us or others? Did we know that we might make decisions and choices we would regret someday?

When I was a young twenty-something, the consequences of my choices weren't even on my radar! I'd be the first to say I pretty much thought I had all the answers. I didn't need anyone to tell me what to do or why. I thought I knew everything I would ever need to know about life.

Life, to me, was meant to be fun. Life meant spending time with friends, living it up, and partying big. My motto was "Don't worry. Be happy." And I wanted to do everything I could before I died. To me, that's what life was meant for—to be lived until you died. Truthfully, why wouldn't I feel that way?

I come from a time when adults didn't talk to children about many things. My parents only shared the good times of their past. While they might have shared what they remembered from the Great Depression, I don't remember my dad sharing a lot, but my mom did talk about raising chickens and having a garden.

But when it came to things that impacted them personally, I really didn't hear about their history. I didn't really know about the choices and decisions they made. Or at least I didn't hear much about the consequences of the decisions or choices they made.

Although, saying that now, I do remember that my dad, as a young man, entered the Air Force to serve his country during World War II. He was a pilot who was shot down over Myanmar (which is now Burma) and was taken captive by the Japanese as a prisoner of war. He was held for eighteen months. But he rarely talked about that time.

What I've found is that men and women who served in whatever capacity then generally will only talk to one another about their experiences. It isn't very often that they share outside of those they served with. To my recollection, my dad only told his story maybe three times after his return. He talked about it twice when I was young, perhaps too young to really understand.

I suppose the consequences for him were that he had to put off going to college at a time when he would have liked to complete school and gone on to become some type of businessman. His dad served as a postmaster general and school superintendent, among other positions. I don't really know what my dad wanted to do with his life. He was active in sports, like basketball. I believe he would have liked to go to college, but I don't recall him saying what he would have majored in. Looking back, there are many conversations I wish we'd had, but didn't.

When the war was over, he got married to his gal from his small-town area. He also stayed in the Air Force and continued his service there. They ended up in Japan, where sadly his wife died of a brain aneurysm, leaving behind a young teenage daughter and a pre-teen son.

My mom had a different life. She went to nursing school in Baltimore, where she grew up. She used to say she had a "gypsy" spirit, meaning she enjoyed traveling, moving, and living in different places. After becoming a nurse, she lived on an Indian reservation for a time in

Oklahoma. She also worked for a doctor in Illinois for a bit.

It was during this time in Illinois that she met my dad and his children, and not too long afterward, they got married. Together, they had three more children. They had the first two in the area where they'd married. Within about five years of their wedding, they relocated to Germany, which is where I was born.

Eventually, my dad was transferred to New Jersey for a few years. After he retired as a Lieutenant Colonel from the United States Air Force, we moved from New Jersey to Maryland, and he went to realtor school. He also took courses that went toward his college education.

At some point, my mom chose being a "wife and mother" over nursing for several years. When I was very young, she nursed for a pediatrician. When I was a preteen, she went back to school to renew her nursing license so she could work in an emergency room, which she did for a few years before she became employed by the Masonic Nursing Home.

The reality is that both of them made choices of varying kinds. They both "paid" consequences that I'll never really know about or understand. Talking about consequences is just not something they shared much about. I know some stories, but I don't know about the consequences of those choices or how they felt about the consequences.

Really, because I never spent time thinking about that, I can't say I ever really considered the consequences I'd face or even how I'd respond to them. I certainly didn't consider the choices and decisions that would actually last decades. It just wasn't a thing for me to think about. So for me, there have been many decisions and choices. They were both big and little, such as picking up that first cigarette, that first joint, drinking that first drink, and even speeding tickets. I also chose to stop attending church (multiple times for multiple reasons throughout my life).

I did not realize that some of those choices would take years to move past. Yet, they are choices I made, decisions I have to live with. Some come with regret. Some with shame. Some, however, come with joy and peace and forgiveness. But again, whether I live with joy and peace today, or have lived with shame and regret, none of that was a factor in why I did what I did.

I'll start with a choice I made when I was roughly six or seven years old, which was that I did not want to attend church any longer. For reasons unknown to me then (and still to this day), my parents decided we would no longer attend the church we were going to. As a child, I had no reason to leave. I liked where we were, and I think we had friends and family who attended as well. But after that choice was made, we went to a different denomination altogether. It was in a different area; we knew no one. I had no friends, and none of my relatives attended.

My brothers (who were two and a half and six years older than me) were given the option to attend church, and they both said they didn't want to go to church any longer. Well, in my obstinate nature (I was the youngest of five, so I was the baby of the family, and admittedly VERY spoiled), I determined I shouldn't have to go either. And for whatever reason, my parents allowed this as well.

It was probably another ten to twelve years before I showed interest in attending church again. And that was because my best friend went every week. I went with her a couple of times and thought it would be "cool" to go with her and "join" her church. I even went through some religious training to join the church.

Unfortunately, it really wasn't a good experience for me as a young person to have. What I heard weekly was that I was a sinner, that I was going to go to hell, and that I had no hope. We would go to church on Friday and pray for the sins we were going to commit that weekend (We had no intention of heading back in there until the following week).

After a time, my thoughts were along the lines of "If I'm going to go to hell anyway, I might as well enjoy myself along the way." I stopped attending church. I was a sinner with no hope, so why go? I made my decision—the merry road to hell it was.

Choices and decisions have a lasting impact. Regardless of when or how they manifest, they will impact you. The biggest question, in my opinion, is, will you recognize that impact?

Will you acknowledge that what is happening is a result of the choices and decisions you've made throughout your life? You may not see it in the days and weeks following the decision. It may take years. It may take decades. But eventually, if you want to heal, you will need to acknowledge your role in what's happening in your life.

"You were taught, with regard to your former way of life, to put off your old self, which is being corrupted by its deceitful desires; to be made new in the attitude of your minds; and to put on the new self, created to be like God in true righteousness and holiness."

Ephesians 4:22-24, TPT

BOUND IN PAIN
AND SELF-HATRED

I always wanted kids. I loved being around babies. My nieces and nephews were the apples of my eye. All my cousins' kids brought joy every time I was around them. They were fun, and I absolutely loved being asked to babysit when I was in my teens. When the children's parents told me they liked having me babysit because I was responsible, I had to do a double take because I really thought of myself as one of the kids. I didn't consider myself "responsible" by any means. That's how connected to them I was.

That was before. When I was young, I was carefree and relatively sin-free, free of the "big" sins anyway. Yes, while I was in high school, I smoked pot, and I stole my parents' cigarettes and smoked them. I stole some of their alcohol when they weren't looking. And I cut classes … well, one class. It was a very boring social studies class (which turned out to be my favorite subject later in life, go figure). I only "hooked" school one full day. I got caught and never did it again.

I was free from the "big" sins, such as murder, adultery, and pornography. That was before I started to party too hard, drink too much, smoke too much pot, and use cocaine. That was before my merry road to hell. That was before I chose to have an affair. Before I chose a promiscuous life. Before I lost my innocence. I really was innocent before that. Or maybe "naïve" is a better word choice. I wasn't a virgin, but not by much.

In all honesty, since what I had heard in the church I attended was that I was a sinner and on the road to hell with little hope for redemption, I figured I might as well enjoy myself along the way. So I made a choice. I partied too hard, I drank too much, I thought only of my own pleasure. I did a few drugs I shouldn't have. The reality of that is that God was watching over me when I didn't even know because I could have, but didn't, become addicted. Perhaps He knew I would have enough trouble headed my way.

It never occurred to me that my actions, my choices, my "merry road to hell" could affect or impact someone else. In my mind, I was going to hell anyway, so what did it matter? It was only affecting me. And who really cared anyway? I sure didn't. At that time, I didn't believe that God cared. Otherwise, why would the pastor of the church say that I was going to hell with no hope?

I wasn't even sure I believed in God. Or, at the very least, the God I believed in was a harsh God, one with no compassion, no love. He was a judgmental God. There was little room for mistakes or errors in judgment and certainly not in the choices that one could make. All I knew about religion (church, Jesus, God, Bible, etc.) was that only a particular church could save me, or that was what I believed then. But it was that church that also told me I was going to hell with no hope because I was a sinner. So, I really didn't have hope in anything nor did I have a desire to know any more about a God that judged me that harshly.

And that was before, in my opinion, I really started sinning.

Within a couple of years, I chose to start a relationship with my boss. I like to think I fell into it, but that would be dishonest. It was a choice. Remember, my

thoughts were, Who cared? I was only hurting myself …
I had no hope. It really didn't matter, and I believed that
my choices were only affecting me.

I liked to think I was "in love," but looking back,
I see that it wasn't love at all. It was sexual, perhaps
lust. It was a secret. Being secretive made it exciting. My
friend, who I had been friends with for half my life called
it what it was—an affair.

It was messy. It was hidden. It was ugly. It was
unnecessary. It was inconsistent. It wasn't safe. Meaning
we didn't practice safe sex. Maybe he thought I was on the
pill, but I was naive. My job was a low-level job, and birth
control was not something that was within my budget.
Truthfully, I'm not sure I even knew what "safe sex" was
at the time. Dumb, naive, call it what you will. Sex was not
something I learned about from my parents. It was not a
subject that we were comfortable talking about.

Little did I realize, at that time, that it wasn't
safe for my heart or for my future. But who knew then
the turn it would take or the years and decades it would
take to even begin to understand the consequences of
those choices?

You probably guessed that I ended up pregnant.
The father of my baby wanted me to have an abortion. I

didn't want that, and he wasn't going to support me, no matter what I said. So I ended up listening to what he was saying and allowed him to convince me that the baby was a mistake.

I believed him when he said my parents wouldn't understand. But really, looking back, how could he know that? He had never met my parents. We didn't even talk about them. Or his family, for that matter. How on earth could he have known how they would respond? But the reality is we were choosing to have an affair.

A secret affair.

Did he just not want a baby? I don't know. He stood to lose many things if our affair came to light. He was in another relationship that probably would have come to an end. He was my boss. I don't expect that would have gone over well then either.

So in the end, I gave in and did what I didn't want to do because I felt like I really didn't have a choice. Or at least, not much of one.

I chose to believe that my parents wouldn't understand. I didn't change that thinking until after they both passed away a few short years later. I realized they actually would have fully supported me, even through the disappointment they would have felt. They would have been my lifeline. I just didn't realize that until it was too late, until they were gone, until I was orphaned.

So, yes, I chose an abortion that I didn't want to have, didn't believe in, and wished could be different.

Because of that choice, I've lived a life filled with shame, regret, despair, self-hatred, and unforgiveness. Unknowingly, I lived bound by that choice. I believed that no one could ever know about the choices that I'd made. I believed that no one would ever understand how I felt. Honestly, I didn't even know how I felt. Even when I started writing this book, I didn't know how I felt.

No one would have ever thought I felt bound to anything because it would have been a greater shame to even admit what had happened, much less, how much I despised myself since I willingly aborted my own baby. I mean, we frequently hear it ... "my body, my choice." Certainly, if you can use those words, you believe and feel them, right? I beg to differ. Some may believe they feel that way. I would point you to behaviors and actions that are likely to tell a different story, regardless of the words that are said.

Throughout my life, I can see where I've felt cornered or attacked and felt the need to defend myself. Truthfully, I likely didn't. Looking at it from a new

perspective today enables me to view my life in a
new context.

I did keep telling myself that it didn't really
impact anyone other than me. I felt like I didn't really
matter anyway ... again, remember, I was going to hell.
I'd only affected myself, but I was so wrong.

How could I feel guilt and condemnation? I
chose that. How could I feel shame and regret? I chose
that. How could I feel unforgiveness? I chose that. I had
so many conflicting emotions within. Sometimes, while
looking back today, I wonder how I was able to put one
foot in front of the other day after day.

It never occurred to me that my future self
would feel anything about this. Never mind how my
future husband would feel. Or how my future kids would
feel. Or how my grandkids (if I was lucky enough to
have some) would feel. I didn't know what my future
friends would feel. Or really, what my friends at that time
thought or felt. None of that mattered. Because, you see,
I was never going to tell anyone what I had done.

It was my shameful secret to keep and not share
with anyone, so why would I think about what someone
else would think? NO ONE WAS EVER GOING
TO KNOW!

Except …

It did impact me. It took me forty-plus years to see that. Looking back, I can see that now.

*"Why was I ever born? My entire life has
been filled with trouble, sorrow,
and shame."*

Jeremiah 20:18, NLT

LIVING
IN WINTER

Seasons change; they come and go. I want to say my abortion happened either in the late fall or early spring. I feel like it took place when there was a change of weather. Honestly, I can easily see myself judging myself because I don't remember the exact date. If it impacted me that much, shouldn't I remember the date or, at least, the season or the year?

Do you ever watch as the seasons change? Spring, where everything comes alive, and it's all new ... buds, flowers, green grass. Even the air smells fresh again.

Then comes summer. With its warmth, fun in the sun, swimming, lazy, hazy days. Days that can feel endless.

Endless until suddenly, fall begins ... where the leaves change color. Flaming reds and oranges before drying out and turning brown. Crisp mornings, temperate days, cool evenings. The smell of fall in the air … not fresh like springtime, but a time of settling in.

This is followed by the bitter chill of winter, which is not my favorite season at all. It's cold, barren, brisk, blustery, and bone-chilling. Even a fireplace doesn't fully warm me up. Yet I lived in that season for most of my life. Living in the cold, feeling the cold.

I'm not sure which part is ugly, uglier, or ugliest. Was it the self-loathing, self-hatred, or shame? Or was it the lies about what a horrible person I was? Or was it what I'd heard and said about and to myself, those things that no one ever said to me, in part, because no one knew?

Was the ugly sitting in the waiting room, seeing all the people there waiting? We all knew what we were there for. It's not like the delivery waiting room at a hospital, where you see the joy of anticipation. Is it a boy? A girl? No, it's not that at all. It's somber faces. Tear-streaked faces. Faces of shame. Faces full of pain. Full of uncertainty.

There are things I remember and things I've deliberately forgotten about that day. I remember arriving at the building and not wanting to go in. I remember entering and being asked if I had someone who would pick me up and drive me home. Because he didn't go in with me, it wasn't clear if I was alone. They wouldn't allow me to drive myself home. I remember wondering if he'd be there to take me back to my car.

Yes, at some point that day, I would have to drive because remember, it was an affair, so taking me home was out of the question. I remember wondering if he'd be there when it was all done. Needless to say, the trust was broken.

I waited in a room with a lot of women. We all pretty much knew why we were there. And we all spent the majority of our time there not really looking at one another as we waited for what seemed like forever before finally being called back. It felt like an eternity, but my name was eventually called.

Everything that happened next showed me that there was a lot of ugliness in the procedure itself.

They asked me, "Are you sure you are pregnant?"

Before I answered, I thought, I mean, really? Would I be here if I wasn't? Or wait. Can I leave now? No, I can't because there isn't anyone here to take me home.

Again, I didn't really feel like I had a choice.

After testing was done to "confirm" the pregnancy, they did a physical exam.

Then, one of the medical professionals came back and said, "Well, we believe you are pregnant, but it's still early. Are you sure you want us to continue?"

Good grief! In my head, I screamed, "No, I don't WANT you to continue. But I don't have a choice! Don't you get it?" I also asked myself, "Do I have a choice? Or do I just not want to face the fact that I have a choice?" After saying that I did want to continue, I was taken into a room where I was instructed to change into a hospital gown. I was repeatedly asked, "Are you sure? How far along are you? When was your last period?"

I didn't know. I wasn't very regular. I just knew that it had been too long in between times.

Then they explained what they would do. I barely remember this, other than I think it was a vacuum aspiration or a suction aspiration or surgical abortion. It's a procedure that uses a vacuum to remove an embryo or fetus (baby!) from the uterus through the cervix. It, at least used to be, a common type of in-clinic abortion that was usually used up to fourteen to sixteen weeks after the first day of the last menstrual cycle. Again, they asked if that was what I wanted. Again, they said I may not be pregnant, but I might be.

Honestly, inside I was saying, "No!" But I also believed I couldn't do this on my own. I remember thinking, No! I don't want an abortion! I don't believe in this. This is wrong. Yet, my words were "Yes." I knew what he wanted. What he said was "best." People wouldn't accept this, wouldn't accept us. It was the early eighties. Black and white didn't go together where I grew up.

I remember that, afterward, when I was telling my friend about it, we said it was like a Hoover vacuum. Not really as a joke, but more as a way of easing the pain. It didn't.

Maybe the ugliness is in the recovery, in hiding the fact that I had an abortion. At work, I was asked, "Why can't you lift that? Just because you don't feel good?"

Then, there were the looks I got. Because, of course, I couldn't tell anyone I'd had an abortion. If I'd done that, I might as well have kept the baby. As I endured the silence, the self-judgment, the suspicious looks, I couldn't help but wonder, Did they know? If so, how did they know? Did they suspect an affair? All I knew was I wanted to get away from there, from everything. But I had nowhere to go.

It took several weeks to recover. Today, after having kids, I realized it was about the same amount of time that I needed to recover from childbirth. Six to eight weeks. No heavy lifting. No sex. Nothing strenuous.

It was painful. Not just in my heart, which was crushed, but also in my body. I still had to work, and even though I had restrictions, one time, I lifted something and nearly passed out because it was too heavy.

Thinking back, I don't believe that secret affair was so secret after all. What reasons would I have for not being able to lift things that I could previously for six to eight weeks while I recovered from a "procedure"? I can't believe I believed people didn't know. Even now I shake my head.

After a time, that affair picked back up, but it wasn't the same. Looking back today, I'm grateful it wasn't. The guilt and shame I felt was overwhelming. I lived it. Every time I saw a child. Every time someone asked me to babysit. I believed that, if they knew what I had done, they wouldn't trust me.

Why would they? I didn't trust myself.

"The human heart is the most deceitful of all things, and desperately wicked. Who really knows how bad it is?"

Jeremiah 17:9, TPT

LAND OF
UGLY WONDERING

I loathed and hated myself. I judged myself. I wondered,
How do I move past this? How long will it take to move
past it? How could anyone understand? Why would
anyone understand? What I believed for years (yes, even
prior to my own abortion), was that the government
sanctioned abortion as a means of birth or population
control. Was this an accurate thought? As far back
as I can recall, at least in high school, this was what I
believed. I can't say I saw it on TV or even was taught
it in high school. Very little was taught regarding sex
education in school. And the reality is, I sure didn't learn
anything from my parents.

Perhaps I believed that since *Roe versus Wade* was
enacted. The Supreme Court said it was ok, so maybe in

my mind, that meant that it was morally okay. That was in 1973, so I would have been a preteen, and I'm sure I would have heard a description from the news.

There must be better options, other methods, that don't involve harming an unborn child. The words "my body, my choice" make no sense to me because I believe life begins at conception. I disagree with those words because it's not just one person's body. I do understand that many people do not want to have a baby. While I understand that, it seems that abortion is a first choice. Maybe I have this opinion because of my own situation, but, when I went to seek an abortion, adoption was never a topic. The problem was the pregnancy. If nothing else, I would have liked to have heard information from the abortion clinic about adoption.

To be truthful, I have had misconceptions regarding why people choose abortion. I know my reason, and while there are a multitude of "personal reasons" for why someone might have an abortion, I also believe there are other options.

Part of the problem around misconceptions is the language we use as we bombard one side or the other with reasons it should or shouldn't exist. And I do believe there are misconceptions on both sides. I think there has been so much "I'm right, you're wrong!" on both sides, that it's nearly impossible for one side to hear the other!

What exasperates me are the sheer numbers. According to the Guttmacher Institute, an estimated 1,038,000 abortions took place in the United States in 2024. This was a less than 1 percent increase from 2023 and an increase of 12 percent from 2020 (www. guttmacher.org).

Yes, I looked a little deeper and found that about 95 percent were "unintended" pregnancies, meaning that about half of those are unwanted, while the other half is a matter of timing. The other 5 percent were for medical reasons (i.e. baby's or mother's health).

More often than not, an unmarried woman is the one having the abortion. It just causes me to question, were alternative options discussed? Forty years ago, there was zero conversation about options, other than, do you want to have this abortion?

I wonder, are life options discussed? Not just for the baby, but are the ramifications of the effects the abortion will have on the mother's life discussed? I don't know if I had a conversation about my future, about how I might have felt, or about how I behaved would have made a difference. I didn't want the abortion to begin with, but to walk forth with the knowledge of how I might feel about myself in the future might have given me some insight into myself that I just did not have.

While I had my abortion while on my "merry road to hell," as I call it, I still believed it was morally wrong. It took me decades, once I started following Jesus to realize that he did not condemn me for that choice. I condemned myself.

Although it was a real struggle, this was where I landed. There must be another solution, aside from abortion first. Why is that the first thought that people have? Get rid of it. But the reality is, you're not "getting rid of it." It will remain a part of you, possibly for decades. It may be a part of your kids' lives (if you have them later). No, really. And it has a name—*microchimerism.* Have you heard of that? I don't think many people are aware of this scientific term.

Basically, with every pregnancy a woman has, cells from each baby are deposited in her body. Essentially, the cells can transfer and become part of the next baby she has. Those cells and DNA can remain in the mother's body for, possibly, decades. It's quite likely that, even if you abort a baby to "get rid of it," you will keep parts of the baby's DNA for a long time. It's probably not as simple as "getting rid of it." I wonder, if people knew or understood the full impact of that, would abortion be the first option for so many?

One profound thought I have is, do people realize the emotional impact this has on the lives of those who choose this option? Many say they don't care. I may have even said it, but I did care. Truth be told, it's taken over forty years to begin to dig deep inside to discover who I am. To discover why I chose what I did and (here's the crux of it) how I feel about it.

What a mess I'd made of my life. I never truly allowed myself to love others. But (I can say this today because I am working through all of this) Jesus commands me to love myself and to love not just God, but others as well. You can certainly care about people, but love them? No, if you don't love yourself, you don't know what love is.

While writing this book, I spent some intensive time in prayer, asking God for a breakthrough from what was blocking me. As I prayed, I felt the Lord telling me that, not only did I not love myself, but that I had hated myself for decades for what I had done. I came upon this verse shortly after that:

"Jesus answered him, 'The first of all the
commandments is: 'Hear, O Israel, the Lord our
God, the Lord is one. And you shall love the Lord
your God with all your heart, with all your soul,
with all your mind, and with all your strength.'
This is the first commandment. And the second,
like it, is this: 'You shall love your neighbor as
yourself.' There is no other commandment greater
than these."

Mark 12:29-31, NKJV

Realizing that I had hated myself for decades
wrecked me. If I hated myself so much, then I couldn't
have really loved anyone else. God, my husband, my kids,
the rest of my family. I felt affection for them, but did I
truly love them the way they should be loved? I realized
my life was a mess because of a lie from decades ago that
impacted my family. The tragedy is they never knew why.
They never knew about the choice I'd made. Or the ways
it impacted me and, thereby, them.

Even today, writing this is hard. I've needed
to learn how to love myself. I've needed to learn how
to love my family. I've made so many mistakes. I was
hard on myself. I needed to be hard on them because I

couldn't allow them to make the same mistakes I'd made. Honestly, I became a control freak. It was "Do it my way, do it the right way, do what I say," or it was silence for them.

I have to say it's taken writing this to come to understand that is how and why I've lived the way I have. I've fought that too. I still don't want to admit how controlling I've been. With God, with my family. Good grief! As I wrote in my diary, I wondered would calling it "Diary of a Mad Woman" or rather "Diary of an Angry Woman" be more accurate? To say I've been angry is not an understatement. I just didn't express it healthily. I thought, "If I hate myself as much as I do, how could anybody like me, if I was real with people?"

I took the anger I had toward myself and turned it toward everyone around me, none of whom deserved that anger. I would take it out on anyone who happened by, who happened to say the wrong thing, or look the wrong way. I spewed anger. I have lived with a great deal of anger. Anger was like a fire inside me, and it had to come out. I didn't know any other way.

"Such a person feeds on ashes; a deluded heart misleads him; he cannot save himself, or say, 'Is not this thing in my right hand a lie?'"

Isaiah 44:20, NIV

WHO'S "LITTLE TIMMY"?

None of us really remember how the name "Little Timmy" came about. We just know that, one day, it was "Where is Little Timmy?" Or "It was Little Timmy's fault." Or "Little Timmy jumped out the window." I've asked, and we don't remember when or why we started that.

But, after so many years without a name, I'm sure Little Timmy was happy to finally know what he was called.

Sometimes I feel sad that my kids didn't know my first child. When the persona of Little Timmy came up, I had mixed feelings. I never said a word about it, but it just felt weird that they would joke about a brother when they didn't even know that was a possibility.

What my kids didn't know was that there was a Little Timmy. A boy who was as much a part of them as they were each other.

"You made all the delicate, inner parts
of my body and knit me together in my
mother's womb. Thank you for making me
so wonderfully complex! Your workmanship
is marvelous—how well I know it. You
watched me as I was being formed in utter
seclusion, as I was woven together in the dark
of the womb. You saw me before I was born.
Every day of my life was recorded in your
book. Every moment was laid out before a
single day had passed. How precious are your
thoughts about me, O God. They cannot
be numbered! I can't even count them; they
outnumber the grains of sand! And when
I wake up, you are still with me!"

Psalms 139:13-18, NLT

Perhaps they "understood" they had a big brother because they could sense the cells from Timmy. I don't know. Remember that thing known as microchimerism?

It's really a fascinating subject. That flow of cells and DNA between mother and child begins to happen early in pregnancy. I had never heard of that. But why would I? I was surely NOT going to investigate anything about a baby from an abortion. To be honest, I probably didn't want to know.

Only recently have I even thought that Timmy could be his name. I've recently paused to think though, How could it not? He was a part of our family that we brought out on trips and when unexplainable things happened. How could it not be a brother they didn't know they had?

I find myself, sometimes, pausing and pondering, what would Timmy have been like? Would he be athletic like his brother? A bookworm like both of his sisters? Organized? Have the heart and memory of them?

What would he look like? Would he be tall or short? What color would his hair be, his eyes? How would he have fit in with our family?

Would he have gone to college? Or trade school? What purpose would God have for him? What kind of brother, or son, would he have been? What would his relationship with his stepfather have been like? Would I have been a good mom to him? What would our relationship have been like? Most likely, I would have been a single mom at a time when that just wasn't a thing.

But mostly, I'm curious what purpose he would have fulfilled. What would God have intended for him? I know that, when I forced God to pivot, that changed my purpose in life. But sometimes, I wonder just what he would have been called to do. We are each so special, and we each have a unique purpose in life.

Birth order is not what it appeared. My kids are boy, girl, girl, boy. But my family is girl, girl, boy. I sometimes wonder, Does that matter? If so, how?

They missed out on watching and playing sports together. Even if there had been seven or so years (or more) separating them, there still would have been things they did together. Board games, soccer, watching football, and celebrating birthdays, Christmas, and other holidays together.

It's funny how, for forty years, I would never have allowed myself the choice to think about these questions. Even now, it makes me nervous. If I'm to heal and help others heal, I feel I need to ask these questions. I need to think about these things and turn these thoughts and feelings over to God. He's a big God, and He can handle what I throw His way.

I think my fear is, what will He give me back? We can become so comfortable with who we've become. Even when we are perhaps not yet the person God has purposed us to be. Releasing everything and allowing God to remold, restore, reset, and redeem means letting it all go, in order to become someone you've never met.

*"For you have acquired new creation life
which is continually being renewed into the
likeness of the One who created you; giving
you the full revelation of God."*

Colossians 3:10, TPT

LIVING WITH
UNSPOKEN SORROW

As stated in the introduction, this book is the story of a part of my life and my journey to redemption only found in Jesus. It's about the choices I made and why. It's the story of an affair that happened; whether it should or shouldn't have been is an altogether different story.

It's about the consequences of actions that were made, that were deliberate, that were chosen. But actions that not everyone wanted. I didn't. But I did it anyway. I didn't know then the impact those choices would have on the rest of my life.

After forty-plus years of walking through life, sometimes I was in deep grief, sometimes in the dark of shame, sometimes in the sorrow of regret, sometimes with seething anger. Oftentimes, my life was all about fun, laughter, and joy. But there was always pain behind it. We oftentimes have no idea what or how others feel, we have no idea the life they've lived, the guilt or shame they may feel.

"Superficial laughter can hide a heavy heart, but when the laughter ends, the pain resurfaces" (Proverbs 14:13, TPT), which was so often true in my case.

Mostly I was able to hide how I felt and who I really was (or at least who I thought I was). I believed that, if people knew the real me, the person who I believed myself to be, they would judge me, hate me, call me a hypocrite. For more than forty years, I believed that. Even when telling dear friends for the first time recently, I have often started the conversation by saying, "Please don't hate me."

Can you blame anyone for hating me? I had a friend in high school who had an abortion. I disagreed with what she'd done. I told her that what she had done was wrong. I'd wondered if she was a slut. If not out loud, I certainly wondered a lot of mean-spirited, judgmental thoughts about her. Our friendship was never the same after that.

I was bound by those thoughts and beliefs for most of my life. Not all of it. But certainly, too long, too many years. And for sure, I believed that I no longer had the right to speak about abortion. I'd had one, so who was I to speak against it? But what I've heard from God is that, because I've had an abortion, I am able and called to speak about abortion. Because I've had one is how and why I know the devastation it can leave in its wake.

The reality is that devastation can be felt by so many. From the baby being aborted to the person having the abortion to the father of the baby to the families of all of these people.

When I say "families," I'm referring to the families currently living, who may have never known (as it was in my case), as well as the future families. And I'm referring to the family I couldn't have dreamt of at that time, the one I didn't think I was worthy of ever having.

And yes, again, even to the father. Although, truth be told, I haven't been in touch with him since I honestly don't know when. I have no idea what impact the abortion of our child had on him. I have no idea if he ever wonders, What if? I'm not sure if that's something I even want to know.

I look back through the years, and I see a journey with many twists and turns. The path has been a mixture of rough and smooth. No one has a smooth path all the time. I've felt very blessed many times in my life. I've also felt much pain in my life.

My parents died in a car accident a few years after I chose an abortion. I never told them about what happened, what I had done. I imagine they wondered what was going on. I know my behavior was off. After the abortion, I'd stayed with him one night. It was late; I didn't think I could drive home. I still lived with my parents in my early twenties. And if I wasn't going home, I always called and let them know, except this one night.

I couldn't call them and tell them. Remember? It was a secret. It was an illicit affair. I passed them as they were taking my mom to work the next day. A wave. That was all I could manage. They never asked. I never told them. I don't think I even apologized.

When they died, I was gutted. I was dependent on them. I missed them then, and I still miss them today. But also, they now knew my secret. There was no more hiding from them. As little as I knew about God or heaven, I did believe that, when we died, we'd know all the bad things we'd done or said, so I wondered, Would they still love me?

I wondered about that for a long time. Even when people told me later that my parents were proud of me, I still wondered. I still felt unworthy.

"Even Gentiles, who do not have God's written law, show that they know his law when they instinctively obey it, even without having heard it. They demonstrate that God's law is written in their hearts, for their own conscience and thoughts either accuse them or tell them they are doing right. And this is the message I proclaim— that the day is coming when God, through Christ Jesus, will judge everyone's secret life."

Romans 2:14-16, NLT

REALIZING
TRUTH

I wish I had talked to my parents. What I think about today is that my parents loved me, regardless of what I'd done. They loved me. Would they have been angry and hurt? Most likely. Would that have stopped them from loving me? Not at all.

What I did was take the opportunity from them to be grandparents to my child. And really, for my children to learn from an older sibling about my parents. Looking back now, I have so many thoughts about that. So many that need self-forgiveness again. Had I kept Little Timmy, he would have experienced my parents as his grandparents here on Earth. He could have shared the kind of grandparents my parents were with my kids today.

Although several of my nieces and nephews did have the opportunity to know my parents as grandparents, we haven't lived near enough for my husband and kids to hear the stories, especially when they were growing up. My nieces and nephews would have "fresher" memories then too.

The night I gave birth to my daughter, she was born by C-section after many hours of labor. It was quiet in the evening, and the nurses brought her to me after I woke up. I remember the wonder I felt the first time I looked at her face. She was beautiful. I felt so unworthy to have her. My mom and dad were gone. Would I know what to do with this precious life I'd been handed? Did I deserve this beautiful baby?

I struggled with my kids growing up, not having the opportunity to know my parents. Honestly, I held my parents on a pedestal. I had watched them as grandparents to my nieces and nephews, and I knew the unconditional love they'd shown. My kids weren't getting that from them! Nor did they have a sibling around to share with them how amazing they were.

I saw how much my parents gave, especially my mom. It breaks my heart when I allow myself to think about not letting them know about their grandbaby from me. It breaks my heart to know that they were gone before my other kids were born.

I feel like I deprived both my children and my parents of that experience. Because even if they had still died, if Timmy had been alive, he could have shared what he remembered of them. As it is, I do believe that they met when my parents died. My mom died first, and in addition to her own family, she was also greeted by Timmy. My dad joined them a few weeks later. Can you imagine their surprise? I imagine they were probably sad that I didn't trust them enough to love me, despite myself.

Weeks before my parents died, I found myself walking into church with them. That was between Christmas and New Year's. It had been years since I'd been in church. They had decided to return to the church we had left when I was about five.

As I already stated, I'm not sure why we left. I do remember having fond memories of that church, especially seeing my cousins there. We would often spend Sunday afternoons with various family members after church. I do believe that had a big impact on my life.

I returned to that church that January, attending with them a couple of weekends. Then on January 22, 1987, we had a blizzard. It was the kind where snow was not measured by the inch, but by the foot. The amounts were higher with the snow drifts, the kind where you cannot open your car doors without shoveling first. I didn't make it home that evening, so the next morning, I had to dig out to go home.

When I got home, I realized my mom, who was a nurse who worked at a nursing home, needed to return to work, where she had already worked a double shift the evening before. The overnight nurse was unable to make it in. After a few hours of sleep, she got up and got ready to return that afternoon. My brother had a snowplow business and had a plow on his truck so he had picked her up, but since I had made it home, my dad decided he would take her back to work.

We knew the route my dad would use to take her to work and the route he would use to come home. About an hour after the start of her shift, we received a phone call from her supervisor asking if my mom was going to be coming in. They had left about two hours before. The drive would normally take about fifteen minutes in clear weather. But since I came home that way, I knew it might have taken thirty minutes, but not two hours.

She didn't make it to work that day because she was killed instantly in a head-on car accident when my father tried to pass a snowplow. Not realizing how much snow was drifting across the road, we believe that he didn't see the oncoming car. Following the accident, my dad was taken to the shock trauma unit of the hospital. That time was such a blur. The shock of realizing she was gone was almost too much to bear. Seeing my dad in the hospital took my breath away. There were times I literally. Just. Could. Not. Go. There.

It was during that time and the months to come that my faith started to grow. I spent days on end, while my dad was in the hospital, learning the Lord's Prayer. Saying, "Not my will, but Yours, Father." I had no idea what to pray for. I felt it would be selfish to pray for him to live. Yet, to lose both of them would be devastating.

I also believed that he would feel crushing guilt after finding out that my mother was dead. And that he was at fault. So, my "baptism" in prayer was turning my earthly father's whole situation over to my heavenly Father.

Thus began the journey of three weeks of not knowing how to pray, what to pray, or what to even think.

There were so many tears. For the first week of his being in the hospital, I went every day. They had told us within the first few days that, because he had so many tubes going into him to help him breathe, for medication, for monitoring, for I-honestly-have-no-idea-what-all-it-was-so-much, they needed to keep the bed moving back and forth so his lungs wouldn't fill with fluid.

During the second week, I could only make it every other day. They were having trouble keeping the bed moving and not having tubing interference. I knew what was going to happen. They had told us that, if they had to stop moving the bed, he would likely get pneumonia. If that happened, his chances of survival would drop.

The third week, I moved into our living room. We had a pull-out sofa bed. I stayed there all day, every day, and all day every day, I learned about prayer. Because I didn't yet understand prayer, and again, I didn't know what to pray for. Ultimately, my prayer became: "I know what I want Lord, but I don't want to be selfish." I felt like I had been selfish my whole life.

"God, what do I pray for? I don't know You, but I'm going to have to trust You!"

During this time, my cousin and her husband, who was a pastor, loved us through all of this. They taught me so much about who God is and how much He cares about His creation. They would stop by and make sure we ate or shared memories of my mom. They were at the hospital before we were on the day of the accident. They were sent by God for sure. I'm forever grateful to them.

Three weeks to the day, and almost to the hour, my dad succumbed to his injuries. It was a combination of relief and reliving that gut-wrenching pain all over again. I was unable to breathe because I was unsure how I would live without the two people I had depended on my whole life.

It became a journey of trying to figure out who I was and who God was/is and would be. I was so comfortable in my life, within the nest of my parents, in their home, with them paying for most of my expenses. Through it all, God showed up.

I'm not blaming Him, although it may sound like I am. What I've learned through the years is that, aside from His Son, God has given us a wonderful gift. It's called "free will." He will not force His will upon us. Even when His plans are so much better for us. We get to choose. My parents certainly had the gift of choosing. My mom's choice was to go to work. My dad's choice was to get her there. This included choosing to try to get her there on time. Unfortunately, for those of us left behind, those were choices we wish they hadn't made. We often don't realize, in the moment, the cost of those choices. We often don't realize until it's too late.

*"Today I have given you the choice between
life and death, between blessings and curses.
Now I call on heaven and earth to witness
the choice you make. Oh, that you would
choose life, so that you and your descendants
might live!"*

Deuteronomy 30:19, NLT

MEMORIES

What we had left of my parents were memories. Many of these memories we shared with others. When we talked about them, we usually started with "Remember when …?" Those memories included laughter. There was the time my mom invited my brother's girlfriend over for pizza and accidentally dropped her cigarette lighter under the pizza on the pan and, yes, into the oven it went. She went crazy looking for that lighter, asking if someone had hidden it from her. Then when it came out of the oven, we were all just astounded that the oven hadn't exploded.

My mom loved to cook, and she did it well. Some of my favorite things she made were dishes she learned while in Germany. I learned how to make apple strudel, which is a hit with many in my family. She made delicious breads, including cinnamon bread and banana nut bread. Christmas cookies of all kinds were a favorite as well. One of the last Christmases she was alive, we got together with our cousins and made dozens of cookies! She could whip up some biscuits and sausage gravy that was absolutely delicious! And blueberry cream cheese pie … my mouth is watering remembering the deliciousness she'd make! Two other things that many loved (I, however, was not one of that many!) were a luscious lemon nut dessert and fruit cake. I was never a fan of either, but I do still periodically get asked for the recipe from someone who remembers loving it.

Today we call it being "crafty," but when I was young, my mom loved to sew and crochet, and she was good at it. She made me a lined wool cape that I still have and a business outfit complete with a jacket, vest, and skirt. She crocheted trivets, blankets, and even a sweater vest for me. She made countless outfits and clothes for my dad.

I asked my family what memories they might have, and I'm sharing them here. Most of these I remember as well.

Mom was called "MomMom." Dad was called "PopPop" by some of the grandkids. Others called them "Grandma" and "Grandpa." They were wonderful grandparents, regardless of the name used! Most of my memories are of them enjoying their children and grandchildren.

After asking others in my family, it made me sad to realize that not everyone remembered them. Several were too young, and some were not yet born. But those that did, remembered PopPop making popcorn. In that respect, my kids received the love of popcorn from my husband because that's something I had forgotten that my dad loved to do!

Or the great milkshakes he would make! Or traveling in his decked-out van with loads of cup holders and seats that swiveled. And the loft in the bedroom where, if you weren't careful, you would bump your head when you climbed the ladder due to a low ceiling.

A few remembered trips they traveled on with my parents. We drove west to my grandparents in Southern Illinois and to the West Coast and took vacations to the beach. Going to Disney for the first time and riding the rides, being scared, but having fun, nonetheless. PopPop in his "Hawaiian" shirts, holding MomMom's hand at the beach.

Spending time at "the house." In their kitchen and the sunroom, eating homemade biscuits and gravy. Or memories of smells such as banana bread being baked, or cooking buckwheat pancakes, or eating homemade and home-churned ice cream! If you didn't sit on the bucket, and take a turn at churning, you might not get some fresh, homemade ice cream! And all the kids loved to be the one that got to do that. And a virgin Sangria-type juice drink made with grape, cranberry, and apple juices, and if memory serves me, it also would have fresh fruit.

Sitting in the living room, watching TV together, playing with our cats. Or outside on the hill behind the house, the old outhouse, the old garage. My mom's grandfather and father built the original house. At some point, her dad expanded the house to what it was when I was growing up.

The house was roughly one hundred years old when we moved there. It was one of a kind. From the basement to the attic and back again, there were always places to hide and places to play!

When we first moved there, we had five bedrooms upstairs. For many, many years, we only had one bathroom. The attic was an unfinished, walk-up that was always cold in the winter. There was always lots of places, areas, furniture, and things to explore.

There were, at least, two dozen stairs leading up to the front porch. We had two entrances into the house.

One entrance was closed off in the hallway, and we had a cedar closet in the hallway there. The other entrance led into our dining room and was the main entrance into the house. We had a huge front yard with a great big walnut tree right next to the sidewalk going to the road. We used to collect walnuts and crack them through the winter. My mom would put them in banana bread and chocolate chip cookies and make all kinds of delicious goodies with them.

The basement had a hard dirt floor with a low ceiling. We used well water, not city water, so we had a sump pump that pumped water into the house. Our washer and dryer were in the basement. Whenever we did laundry, we had to make sure that we didn't do a large load. Not because of the washer, but because of the pump's capacity! We'd have to stand downstairs while the washer filled with water. We did this so that we could turn it off occasionally so the pump wouldn't run out. Then, we'd go back during the rinse cycle. If we forgot ... well, read on to learn about what happened when we forgot something.

Forget taking a shower or flushing the toilet at the same time! That was, for sure, a disaster in the making! Flushing while showering would freeze you in the shower (you were allowed to forget ONE time, but after that, all bets were off, and you got in trouble)! But to do all three at once meant water would stop pumping. Don't ask me why. I did ask about that but never received a satisfactory answer. If you know why, please let me know. It didn't matter if you were in the middle of washing your hair and had shampoo in your eyes, when the water stopped, you had to go get the water (we called it a "sump pump" back then) working again.

The pump was in the basement, in a crawl space. And when it went out—oh, wow—what a hassle it was to crawl in there and have to jigger with whatever that thing was called to get it cut back on. After twenty-plus years living there, I never remembered the name of that doodad. All I knew was that there were spiders, likely snakes, and all kinds of scary creatures. It was a pain to get that thing back on! Whenever the pump went out, we'd have to wait for it to refill to use it again.

Despite its quirks, I loved that house, but I've never lived anywhere that didn't have city water since then. For years, my parents talked about drilling another well, but I think the cost held them back.

Some more memories my nieces and nephews have are of hearing my dad on the CB radio talking with

truckers, telling them about being a POW, and how he
held no ill will toward the Japanese. Plus, in his view,
"they make the best cars." He owned a Volvo for a long
time, but when it came time to "upgrade," he bought a
Toyota and never went back!

More memories included "eating Klondike bars
or watching MomMom sew." I remember a plaid suit
she made for my dad. He wanted the plaid to match the
entire suit, both the pants and the coat, and she did it.
She loved to sew. I still have a lined wool cape that she
made for me. I have fond memories of the bridesmaids'
dresses she made for my brother's wedding, as well as her
dress. She also knitted and crocheted.

Her garden was amazing. It was probably half
as wide as a football field and easily half as long as one,
if not longer. She would plant all kinds of vegetables.
Tomatoes, peppers, beans, corn, squash, melons, and she
even branched out to strawberries and blueberries. We
could take an ear of corn and drop it in a pot of boiling
water for like five minutes, pull it out, slather butter on
it, and have the best ear of corn you'd ever eaten! Fresh
from the garden.

She once grew a pumpkin that weighed over
one hundred pounds. We ended up winning a trip to

Transylvania, Romania and a visit to Dracula's castle.
She, my brother, and I went. Our trip lasted from late
October through early November. It was the year Jimmy
Carter was elected president of the United States. That's
all the people in Romania talked about. While we were
there over our holiday, Halloween, they don't celebrate it
(or didn't at that time), like we do. So while we had hoped
to be at "Dracula's Castle" for Halloween, I believe we
were not able to be there. It was a fascinating trip. But
also, a story for another time.

When we traveled on trips, we usually rode in a
camper or van. In 1974, my dad had "decked out" our
green van … I know the van was green, because that's
the photo album title. The first bit of the trip was a
family reunion in Kentucky, even though my dad was
from southern Illinois. I think we met up with some
family; I know we have a picture of my grandfather and
step-grandmother behind the tombstones of his mom
and dad, so I believe they were his parents.

From there, we passed through the arch in St.
Louis, Missouri, on to Nebraska and stopped at Little Big
Horn and saw where Custer's Last Stand took place. The
next part of our journey was through the rugged country
of the Badlands in South Dakota to Mt. Rushmore and

on into "historic" Flintstones Land (I guess also known as Bedrock City), where we encountered Pebbles, Bamm-Bamm, and Dino the dinosaur. LOL. Our next stop was Devils Tower in Wyoming before we spent some time at Yellowstone National Park. We saw lots of wildlife, Old Faithful, and the Mammoth Hot Springs.

We then spent a bit of time at Grand Teton National Park, before we journeyed on to meet up with "family" in American Falls, Idaho. We had met or learned about them at the family reunion in Kentucky, and they invited us to stop by on our trip. After spending time with our "cousins," we continued to Brigham City, Utah, where we watched a reenactment of the last spike being driven into the railroad connecting the East Coast to the West Coast.

Then came what has become my favorite place on Earth. We stopped at the Grand Canyon. I would honestly love to live there. It's that beautiful. Now when I think about the Grand Canyon, I am just in complete awe that God would create such a place for His people. We also traveled to Bryce Canyon, which is additional beauty to me.

I cannot leave out the Painted Desert and the Petrified Forest National Park in Arizona or the Great Sand Dunes National Park and Preserve in Colorado. All just beautiful! Then we got to Royal Gorge in Colorado. Oh, my! I was not comfortable with how high that bridge was! I also had the opportunity, along the way, to stand in four states at once! Four Corners in New Mexico, Utah, Colorado, and Arizona. It's fun to say, "I visited four states all at the same moment!"

I remember, on one of our trips, my mom was cooking on a campfire cookstove, and she was going to use her cast iron skillet on it. It had been freezing that night. My mom had placed her pan toward the outside of the van. When she placed it over the fire, the pan cracked right down the middle.

Other trips included going to Montana, Nevada, Washington, Oregon, British Columbia, Mexico, Colorado, and Wisconsin. In all the time they were alive, the only two states we, as a family, did not visit were Alaska and Hawaii. To my knowledge, they did not ever get to Alaska; however, I was able to send them to Hawaii on a wonderful trip about two years before they passed.

These are all journeys that I wish their grandchildren could have had with my parents.

It took many years to come to accept that my kids did have good grandparents in my husband's family. They were well-loved and treated very well. Letting go of what could never be was a lesson that broke my heart. But in some ways, it also cleansed my heart. It helped me to see the living grandparents in a different light and to accept them in wonderful ways.

Perhaps, they were not the same as my parents, but they gave them a love of books (Their grandmother worked at a bookstore and always had books for them). She was German, and she cooked a lot of German food. This birthed a love of bratwursts, *rouladen*, and *knödel*. For those unfamiliar with these dishes, you'll want to become familiar! Rouladen is thinly sliced beef, with spicy mustard spread over it, sprinkled with salt and pepper, some sliced onion, a piece of bacon, and a slice of dill pickle. Roll that up, put it in a baking dish, add water (to make yummy gravy), and bake until tender and nearly falling apart. Knödel is not nearly as easy as the rouladen, unless you do as I do and buy the powdered mix in a box. Just make sure you follow English directions or you may get the measurements incorrect. Ask me how I know that! But knödel is basically a ball that's made up of potato flakes, that you boil in a large pan. My kids grew up calling them softballs. Because of the time investment, we typically made these meals for special occasions, such as birthdays and holidays.

They also went fishing with their grandfather, where they learned about life around the water and snow. They shared a love of the outdoors, gardens, plants, and animals, especially dogs. Their grandfather and nana lived on the lake so they learned about boating and fishing as well.

"I promise that I will never leave you helpless or abandon you as orphans—I will come back to you!"

John 14:18, TPT

LEARNING
TO TRUST

My first pregnancy was the result of an affair. Someone else may get pregnant from being raped. Someone may choose abortion because of testing and discovering a defect. Some also choose abortion as a means of birth control.

There are many reasons people have abortions. There are many emotions and feelings that manifest after having an abortion as well. If I had known then how I would feel forty-plus years later, I'm not sure I would have chosen abortion. Regardless of how the father felt.

For me, it felt like I'd murdered my child. No one told me that, but that was what I believed. I chose it, and I'm sorry that I did. If I could choose again, I would choose life for my child. Whether that was life with me or life with another family, I would choose life. I sometimes wish someone would have told me what I would feel through the years. I wish someone had told me about the turmoil I would live through and that that would lead to so many more negative emotions.

I have discovered that how I felt about myself impacted my life. It has impacted how I treated my family, my friends, and my co-workers. I have had a hard time trusting people. I think that, in part, stems from not trusting myself. How could I trust myself when it was always my view that abortion was wrong, but I did it anyway?

I didn't think I could handle having a child. I didn't trust myself. At all. And if I can't trust myself, who can I trust? Certainly not my parents, siblings, spouse, kids, or co-workers. If I'm not trustworthy, no one is.

Regardless of how someone gets pregnant, the choice made from that pregnancy will surely impact their life. I do find it interesting that, even though I didn't grow up in the church, I carried the belief that abortion was wrong. I cannot say where that belief came from, unless it was an unspoken belief my parents had. They did love children. I suppose that love rubbed off on me.

I only knew of one person prior to my abortion that had an abortion. Like I said, I judged her. She wasn't one I was going to turn to in order to discover a different route in life. I am sorry today that I was hateful toward her. And the reality for her, if I remember, I think she thought her parents would kill her. Would they have really killed her? That's an interesting question.

I'm sure, at that time, we believed that was a possibility. I thought my parents would hate me and disown me. I was wrong. I like to think now that, if that was her thought, she was wrong as well.

Truthfully, I hear that a lot when, especially teenagers, think their parents will be angry at them for something: "My parents would kill me if [fill in the blank]." I admit, I can't say that every time I have heard that, I told that teen they were wrong. Whether the omission was to allow that fear to prevent the teens from doing something unwise or not, I can't answer today. Looking back on my life, I want to share with them how what they are doing might impact their life. That nothing will separate them from that love of a parent.

I do believe that today, as in ancient times, child sacrifice, regardless of the age of the child, is against God's desire. I believe that it grieves God's heart. He is Creator. He is Love. We don't know love if we don't know Him. He created us, and He has a purpose and a plan for each of us. In the verse at the end of this chapter, the NKJV uses the phrase "For I know the thoughts that I think toward you." The Lord thinks of His plans for you. Good and marvelous plans. Regardless of the choices you've made. Regardless of what you've done, or not done, He thinks of you. They are good thoughts. He has a plan and purpose for your life.

"Here's what Yahweh says to you: 'I know all about the marvelous destiny I have in store for you, a future planned out in detail. My intention is not to harm you but to surround you with peace and prosperity and to give you a beautiful future, glistening with hope. When you call on me and come to me in prayer, I will listen to your every word.'"

Jeremiah 29:11-12, TPT

THE JESUS
JOURNEY

All believers have what I call a "Jesus Journey." Jesus chose to take on our sins, whatever those sins were. He chose to take them on. He chose the cross for us. He chose forgiveness for us. We all have to start from somewhere, something, or someplace where we need and yearn for forgiveness.

The differences between us all lie in the journey. There is a path that each of us walk along, and Jesus is with us always. When are our eyes open to Him beside us, within us? Where do we see the redemption from Him? That's the journey. We may have a similar abortion journey, but how you've walked it out and where and when you felt that forgiveness and redemption will differ from my path.

Perhaps your journey to forgiveness and redemption has nothing to do with abortion. It will still be a journey. Even those who have walked with Jesus all their lives will have some type of Jesus Journey. Age does not dictate the time of the journey. As I say, some will have walked with Jesus all their lives. Every journey is different. There was a time I thought that walking with Jesus from early on was an easier path. It's not.

Because we live in a world where humanity has fallen, where God blessed us with free will, we will need to live and work alongside humanity. We all get to make choices. As I said earlier, while we may think our choices only impact ourselves, I don't believe that. We may never know how our choices impact others. Obviously, my parents couldn't know while they were here on Earth how their choices that day would impact their kids. But those choices impacted each of us in different ways.

What's important is that you come to recognize and realize that Jesus died for you too. Again, whatever your sin is, whatever "unforgivable" thing you did. It is forgivable. It's forgiven.

In the past, I've had many skewed thoughts about God and Jesus as well. I thought they were both harsh and judgmental. I thought I was going to hell, no matter what I did and no matter how I tried to overcome my sins. All I knew about the Holy Spirit was that He was some type of "ghost." I'm not trying to diss the church here, but I feel like we can and should do better with helping people come to the Trinity.

Today I'm living my life in the light of His forgiveness. In the light of Jesus "who for the joy that was set before him endured the cross, despising the shame, and is seated at the right hand of the throne of God" (Hebrews 12:2, NKJV).

Joy. Jesus accepted the cross for the joy of setting me free from my sins (I'll share more on this a little later). You see, I believed I could never be forgiven for taking a life because, to me, that is what happens with abortion.

I don't know how many times I read Hebrews 12:2 before I got a true glimpse into what this meant. It made me bawl my eyes out. The following is a notation from *The Passion Translation* that hit me so hard when I read this, and it helped me see Jesus from yet another light.

Jesus chose ME as the JOY set before him. He DESIRES me to the point of laying down his life. He PURSUED me; He DID NOT SEE my weaknesses and failures ... He only SEES what I WILL BE!! That COMPLETELY WRECKS me!!! How can I think less of myself, when He LAID HIS LIFE DOWN FOR ME? We (I) cannot dishonor Him that way.

"We look away from the natural realm and we focus our attention *and expectation* onto Jesus who birthed faith within us and who leads us forward into faith's perfection. His example is this: Because his heart was focused on the joy of knowing that you would be his. "Instead of the joy set before him," "his was the joy of our salvation. He placed before his eyes the bliss we would forever share together with him, which empowered him to go through his agony. Instead of remaining in heaven's glory with the Father and all the angels, he chose you as the joy set before him. He desires you to the point of laying down his life and being God for all eternity to be with you. He pursued you, not seeing your weakness and failures but what you will be. He can see what we will be in the end from the beginning. This was the joy that prompted him to become a man. He endured the agony of the cross and conquered its humiliation, and now He sits exalted at the right hand of the throne of God!" (Hebrews 12:2, TPT).

My heart! Every time I read that, I see it anew. Jesus not only loves me beyond what I can imagine, I am His JOY. Think about that.

What I find really amazing the longer I reflect in and on this is that it isn't just a message for me. It is for YOU as well! YOU are His JOY!

Why isn't this shouted everywhere? I don't know! I wasn't taught this, so I didn't know to share it. But for goodness' sake, and I do mean for GOODNESS' SAKE; this is a message we need to share! That we have not been taught this is NO reason to not share it! He set me before Him and finds joy in me. He set YOU before Him and finds joy in you too! It's crazy for us not to share!

"These things I have spoken to you, that My joy may remain in you, and that your joy may be full."

John 15:11, TPT

While my faith at that time wasn't strong and I didn't have much knowledge and even less wisdom and understanding, I did believe some things. I did believe that heaven was real. It's the place we go when we die, where we will be reunited with our loved ones.

I did believe that everything we ever did would be on full display for others to see. And truthfully, even my journey isn't without several stops and starts. I'd go to counseling and forgive myself. I'd walk through how

I felt, and after a bit of time passed, I'd be back into the spiral of unforgiveness. The most difficult emotion to come against was the self-hatred I felt.

I realized recently how much I still felt that way about myself. While writing this book, I looked at myself in a different light. I can see that I have felt that self-loathing. When I would start to explain my story to someone, I would start by saying, "Please don't hate me." It occurred to me that the reason I would start that way was because I hated myself for what I had done.

As I was studying one day, I came across this passage of Jesus answering the question of what Old Testament commandment is the greatest. It hit me in a whole new light. Understanding was dawning. I cannot love God or my neighbor if I don't love myself. Ouch! That hurt. Probably the hardest for me, and the one I am called to the most.

"Then the LORD answered me and said,
'Write the vision
And engrave it plainly on [clay] tablets
So that the one who reads it will run.
For the vision is yet for the appointed [future] time

It hurries toward the goal [of fulfillment];
it will not fail.
Even though it delays, wait [patiently] for it,
Because it will certainly come; it will not delay."'

Habakkuk 2:2-3, AMP

Why is this the hardest? Because really, it's not always me talking. It's God calling me to invite others to redemption, to forgiveness. It's sharing with people that, although the journey may be hard and although it may seem as though there is no forgiveness, it's a journey worth walking through to get to the other side.

I get it, if you don't talk about it, it will just go away. But the reality is, it doesn't go away. It will eat you alive if you let it. Sharing the journey may initially sound like you're sharing your shame, but you are not sharing the shame because there is no shame. God isn't shaming you. Even your kid isn't shaming you. Sometimes we like to think that there is only shame.

But that's not God in your head. That's the enemy trying to keep you away from God. God is here to love us and have a relationship with us. He's not here to blame and despise us. If that were the case, then Jesus would have had no reason to come to Earth.

But he did come to Earth. He did so to save us from ourselves. We haven't done a great job of preaching that, neither the people nor the church. God sent His son, Jesus, who came to Earth willingly, to restore our relationship. And we are called to spread that news. But what we hear, or are taught, or at least what I heard, was that I was a sinner going to hell. The enemy has a field day with those proclamations. If that continues to be taught, we will likely turn away from God. But Jesus came so that we could have life, an abundant life!

"The thief does not come except to steal, and
to kill, and to destroy. I have come that they may
have life, and that they may have it
more abundantly."

John 10:10, NKJV

Even though I was invited to write my story, I fought it. I really could not tell you how many times I said "no." It was a lot. But God He kept nudging me. He kept reminding me that He loved me, that my story was one that needed to be shared. My story could make all the difference to that one person who is thinking of having an abortion, but doesn't really want to. For that person who has the answer to end abortions, but perhaps doesn't realize it yet. Perhaps they have an answer but think that people really don't care and don't want the answer. To those people, I say, "Yes, we are here for you. To support you. To give you options. Let's talk."

I was called to write because God has a vision of a safe place for all His children.

> "Love the Lord your God with all your heart
> and with all your soul and with all your mind
> and with all your strength. The second is this:
> 'Love your neighbor as yourself.' There is no
> commandment greater than these."
>
> Mark 12:30-31, NIV

God is my strength; He's the solid foundation of love in my life. Without Him, I cannot love Him, myself, my family, or anyone else. What makes me so emphatic in stating this?

I've inwardly questioned for years if I could truly love my kids if I took the life of my firstborn. How could I love like Jesus if I did that? Because I have the gift of faith and because He is my strength, my foundation; then yes, it is possible!

Writing this book has helped me look back over the years and see some areas where God was a certain presence. After my parents died, I remember the days I would go to the chapel where my cousin's husband was associate pastor. There were many times he would open it so I could go in to pray, well, wail was more like it. I cannot begin to describe the times I would lay on the bench and cry just gut-wrenching sobs. Today, I still have leaky eyes. I would have a need to spend time with the Lord, so I'd call my cousin, and he'd open it up for me. I needed God/Jesus/Holy Spirit so badly. I'd cry until I couldn't cry any longer.

Then a couple of years later, God was present when I married my husband in that same chapel. The joy of moving forward. Walking with the Lord, another step in the Jesus Journey.

After my first girl was born, I realized that I needed to be in church again. Even though we lived in Germany at the time, we had access to the military base's chapels. So, we started going, and once again, there was God. I was feeling lonely and scared as a new mother. I felt unqualified and unfit, but there was God, placing people in my life yet again.

When we moved back to the United States from Germany, well, that was interesting. We had come home for the Christmas holidays. I had both my girls by then and was pregnant with my last child. My husband was going to be on assignment in South Korea for a few weeks, so I was staying in the states until he was done. He was also applying for jobs stateside so we could move back. I was getting lonely for family and really needed help with my kids. They were two, one, and one soon-to-be-born. Yes, I had three children, each one year apart. That's for another story though.

After my husband left for Korea, he received a job offer. Could he start in something like two weeks? It would take him a few days to get back to Germany. I could meet him after he got there, but he'd have to leave most of the house to me to get packed up or sell what we weren't bringing to the states. I did not want to have to pack up the house in Germany by myself, so I flew back before he did. Yes, by myself with my nearly two and nearly one-year-old daughters.

God was with me. I did ok on the plane by myself, but as we were getting closer to landing, I started to become concerned about how I was going to get us all off the plane by myself and through customs with all our luggage too. Well, God had a soldier right there for me. He was single, but he could see I was struggling. He stayed with me until I got through customs. One of my husband's co-workers was there to meet me and take me to our house.

God was, for sure, with me there. No one thought I could get the house packed up and things sold within two weeks. But they didn't know God or me when I set my mind to something. I got everything sold and the movers to the house with a day or two to spare. Never mind the argument I had with the soldier that wanted to buy the kitchen sink that had been clearly marked not for sale. It wasn't mine to sell, you see. If it had been, he could have had it. There again, another soldier came to my rescue. God had placed people in my life when I needed them. Oh, and there was the stereo component that I misunderstood and sold. But my husband has mostly forgiven me for that now. At least we can chuckle about it some decades later.

We found a house and lived closer to our family for nearly three years. Then we learned that my husband's company was going to move him. We would be moved either to North Carolina or to Texas. Well, I had heard about the tornadoes in Texas and made the statement, "Not even God could get me to that tornado state of Texas!" If you ever want to laugh at your plans and how life unfolds, go ahead and tell God what even He can't make you do. It did take two years though. First, we moved to North Carolina, and while we were there, we met another wonderful church family, along with neighbors, and became good friends. We lived there for two years. The second spring we lived there, we had tornado warnings nearly every day for about a month. It was crazy. It felt like every time we turned around, there was another warning.

One week, I was out walking with my friend, and she was telling me she was going to have to move. They had been renting their house, and the owners were moving back. They needed to find another home. They had been looking, but had been unable to find another home with their floor plan, or one like our house. That weekend, my husband and I were talking. He was on a business trip to Europe, and he mentioned that his company indicated we were going to have to move again. Guess where we would have to move. Yep. Texas was in our future, unless my husband planned on finding another job. After living through a month of tornado warnings, I chuckled and said, "Well, I already have the house sold, so I guess we're moving!" Yes, our neighbor bought our house. We moved out at about the same time they needed to move. I didn't have to sell or clean anything. She took care of the cleaning as they were moving in. God was all over that move. I could go on and on about the number of times God has placed people and opportunities in my life. These aren't just a few of those times; there are so many more.

As I have thought through writing this book and have now spent every day journaling and spending more time with the Lord, I've discovered that there is so much holy joy in seeing scripture come to life and understanding it in such a different light!

*"And I pray that he would unveil within
you the unlimited riches of his glory and
favor until supernatural strength floods your
innermost being with his divine might and
explosive power. Then, by constantly using
your faith, the life of Christ will be released
deep inside you, and the resting place of his
love will become the very source and root of
your life."*

Ephesians 3:16-17, TPT

SAFETY
AND FREEDOM

It's tough to say, but I know I made a choice. I didn't have to have an abortion, even if someone else said I did. I could have said no. I do regret that, but what I'm realizing is that, although I made that choice and sometimes have condemned myself for that choice, God didn't, Jesus didn't, and the Holy Spirit didn't. And the bottom line is that those are whose opinions matter. It doesn't even matter what I think.

I realized this one day when I was studying my Bible and read Hebrews 12:2 in TPT: "Because his heart was focused on the joy of knowing that you would be his, he endured the agony of the cross and conquered its humiliation..." followed by a note in that version that said, "He desires you to the point of laying down his life and being God for all eternity to be with you. He pursued you, not seeing your weakness and failures but what you will be. He can see what we will be in the end from the beginning. This was the joy that prompted him to become a man."

I mean seriously. That blew my mind. He came to Earth to be tortured and die on the cross for my sins, and He did it with joy. What?!? Who does that? God in the form of Jesus, His Son. That's who. Someone who loves me beyond my understanding.

That's not a judgmental God. This is a Jesus who loves me so much that He came to Earth and suffered for me! This is the Holy Spirit who isn't a ghost at all. He is a Helper whom Jesus sent after He died to guide us and intercede (pray to God) for us. To give us understanding, clarity, and wisdom.

Then I read Jeremiah 29:11 (NIV), which so many may know this version of that verse: "I know the plans I have for you…". However, in the NKJV, it says, "For I know the THOUGHTS that I think toward you, says the LORD, thoughts of peace and not of evil, to give you a future and a hope."

His desires toward me and thoughts toward me are good desires and thoughts. Ok, first, He THINKS about me. Can we just pause there and think about that? He knows the THOUGHTS He thinks toward us. Secondly, those thoughts are of peace, not evil (regardless of what we think of ourselves, He does not think evil of us!), and He thought to give us a future and hope.

He does not think about my failures and flaws, but of what I will become! That joy, that knowing, and that thinking of me is why He sent His Son to become a man who ultimately would give His life for me. He's done the same for you.

Imagine that. No, really. Pause and think about that for a minute. He's not looking to judge me (or you). He's thinking of who I will become. He's thinking of who YOU will become. He's thinking about the book that was written about me before I was born. He's thinking about that book written about you before you were born. He's thinking about the book written for my aborted baby before he was born too. Remember that? His precious thoughts about us cannot be numbered, nor counted, because they are more numerous than grains of sand! That is not a judgmental God, nor a Jesus who condemns, nor a Holy Spirit who doesn't care.

That's a God who creates and loves, a Jesus who for JOY came to Earth to take my sins upon Himself and be beaten to death so that I might be forgiven and send me a Helper and Guide in the Holy Spirit after death.

When God sees you, He sees joy! He doesn't see anything you may have done wrong. He had joy in going to the cross for you as well.

Maybe you've heard this before. But maybe you didn't grasp that it was possible. That's where I was. I had heard parts of this.

But the understanding was sorely lacking. I'm not sure if it was ingrained from being told I had no hope or what. But it's taken me years to accept that I am enough, that I am a delight to God.

In His arms is the safest space to be.

"The name of the Lord is a strong tower;
The righteous run to it and are safe."

Proverbs 18:10, NKJV

I am now free to be who God made me. I am redeemed. I am forgiven. I am His child. I am chosen. I am loved. I am whole. I am brave. I am wise. I am a light for the world.

I think before I speak. I speak words of love and kindness. I speak truth. I am free and I am brave. I can speak the truth of my life without shame. I can speak of the decimation of my life without guilt. Because of all God has done to save me. He created me. He sent His Son to take the punishment for me. He and His Son sent the Holy Spirit to help guide me, to teach me how good and right and true God is.

> "But he was pierced for our rebellion,
> crushed for our sins.
> He was beaten so we could be whole.
> He was whipped so we could be healed."

Isaiah 53:5, TPT

I recently had some prayer time with the Lord and was brought to Ezekiel 47:1-12, which shows a river that starts with a trickle, then you follow along a little and the water is shallow and ankle deep. Before you know it, you're wading in knee-deep water until you go a little further, and then it's waist-high. And suddenly, God has that river of grace flowing over you so deep you can't swim!

What did that do? The riverbank now has an abundance of trees on each side of the river. The river is flowing into the stagnant waters of the Dead Sea and making that water become fresh water where fish can thrive and healing happens. The trees on the riverbanks are filled with fresh fruit that is good to eat.

This. This is my spirit today. This is my soul today. This is my body today. Forgiven. Redeemed. Healing. Loving. Free. Strong.

When you're feeling cut off, not seeing life signs, follow Habakkuk 3:18 (NKJV): "Yet I will rejoice in the Lord, I will joy in the God of my salvation." He is waiting with open arms and will lead you through. Trust that He will strengthen you.

*"But continue to grow and increase in
God's grace and intimacy with our Lord
and Savior, Jesus Christ. May he receive
all the glory both now and until the day
eternity begins. Amen!"*

2 Peter 3:18, TPT

JOURNAL
THROUGH TIME

The following are thoughts that I had before I even began writing this book. The struggle has been real. It has taken time to work through all of this. A faith coach suggested that I start journaling. Not necessarily to write a book, but just to get my thoughts down. That is, in part, why this section will seem disjointed. It is because I was.

Journaling was not normal for me; in fact, it's taken several years for me to write in a journal regularly. I didn't understand what the point would be.

I may have sensed at that time that I was called to write this book, but I surely did not want to. At all. I was defiant in NOT writing this.

Early on, journaling was day to day. Triumphant one day, struggling the next. Confidant one day, timid and fearful another. What I am learning through this process is that I have no regrets spending time every day with our Father. I find joy in becoming closer to God daily. Having been given knowledge of who I am because of the Son has changed my perspective of myself. I have caught glimpses of the struggles I've had year to year, yet I have been strengthened to find the verses and words to help me walk out the truth, and being able to share that with others has been such a blessing.

The following verses from 2 Samuel are of David's reflection of his life. On this day, they hit me in such a different way. I felt almost a kindred spirit with David. From God being my shelter, my refuge, my strength of feeling I had been delivered from not only my enemies, but I was starting to be delivered from myself as well.

It's not been an easy journey. However, it is a journey that is well worth traveling. Again, having the knowledge that, after winter, comes spring is so comforting.

MAY 20, 2022

Me. Who am I? How did I get to where I am? I don't
even know if I have the answers. I know that I am a child
of God. I know that, despite myself, He loves me. He
created me. He knows my steps. In fact, He knows the
steps I'll take before I do. Did He maybe hope I'd make
different choices? I'm sure He did. I'm sure He wanted
me to follow His ways all my days. But I had other plans.
I had other thoughts. I thought I knew better. I usually
do. Oh, how the irony of that impacts me. I've made
some great choices in my life. Following Him (finally).
Listening (finally) when He called me and led me to
where I am now.

I've had far more choices that haven't been so
good. Many have been ones that I've deeply regretted.
They are also choices that cannot be undone in any way.

"The LORD is my rock, my fortress and my
deliverer; my God is my rock, in whom I take
refuge, my shield and the horn of my salvation.
He is my stronghold, my refuge and my savior—
from violent people you save me. I called to the

LORD, who is worthy of praise, and have been saved from my enemies."

2 Samuel 22:2-4, NIV

"The waves of death swirled about me; the torrents of destruction overwhelmed me. The cords of the grave coiled around me; the snares of death confronted me. In my distress I called to the LORD; I called out to my God. From his temple he heard my voice; my cry came to his ears. They trembled and quaked, the foundations of the heavens shook; they trembled because he was angry."

2 Samuel 22:5-8, NIV

"He reached down from on high and took hold of me; he drew me out of deep waters. He rescued me from my powerful enemy, from my foes, who were too strong for me. They confronted me in the day of my disaster, but the LORD was my support. He brought me out

into a spacious place, he rescued me because he
delighted in me."

2 Samuel 22:17-20, NIV

"You save the humble, but your eyes are on the
haughty to bring them low. You, LORD, are my
lamp; the LORD turns my darkness into light.
With your help I can advance against a troop;
with my God I can scale a wall. As for God, his
way is perfect; The LORD's word is flawless; he
shields all who take refuge in him. For who is
God besides the LORD? And who is our Rock
except our God? It is God who arms me with
strength and keeps my way secure. He makes my
feet like the feet of a deer; he causes me to stand
on the heights."

2 Samuel 22:28-34, NIV

I'd rather write anything than this. But I can't
because this is my story. Like it or not, it's what I've
experienced. It's part of my history. But it doesn't

define who I am today or who I have become because I know my God, because I am living my life forgiven and beloved, having been shown mercy and grace.

I know that my child forgives me. My mother forgives me.

By stepping out in belief and looking at what I believe God considers sacred and the choices I've made, there are times I can relate really well to David. He was someone after God's heart. God considered him righteous. I won't say God has always called me righteous before I knew who He was, or maybe He did, and it just took a long time before I knew or understood what "righteous" meant. Heck, I'm still figuring that one out! I'm a forgiven sinner. Forgiven by the blood of the Lamb. Forgiven because Jesus chose to take my sin upon Himself on the cross. Some days, it's easier to reconcile having an abortion than other days. Some days, it's easier to say I'm a forgiven sinner than it is on other days. Some days, I just want to leave my head buried in the sand and act like it never happened.

But it did. And yet, I am washed in the Blood of the Lamb and so grateful to be so.

"Oh, give me back my joy again; you have broken me—now let me rejoice. Don't keep looking at my sins. Remove the stain of my guilt. Create in me a clean heart, O God. Renew a loyal spirit within me. Do not banish me from your presence, and don't take your Holy Spirit from me. Restore to me the joy of your salvation, and make me willing to obey you. Then I will teach your ways to rebels, and they will return to you."

Psalms 51:8-13, NLT

Jesus is the joy of my salvation. Without Him, I am literally nothing. With Him, I can stand against the arrows of those who will judge me. Who will consider me less than. Who will not believe me. Who will hate me for my stand. Who will not understand me. But I will stand firm in the calling that I have. I will have the belt of truth around my waist. I will place the breastplate of righteousness squarely in front of me. I will wear the shoes of the gospel in peace. But my faith will repel those arrows. I will have the helmet of salvation and the sword of the Spirit. Praying in all things. On all occasions. In all ways. For all.

"Finally, be strong in the Lord and in his mighty power. Put on the full armor of God, so that you can take your stand against the devil's schemes. For our struggle is not against flesh and blood, but against the rulers, against the authorities, against the powers of this dark world and against the spiritual forces of evil in the heavenly realms. Therefore put on the full armor of God, so that when the day of evil comes, you may be able to stand your ground, and after you have done everything, to stand. Stand firm then, with the belt of truth buckled around your waist, with the breastplate of righteousness in place, and with your feet fitted with the readiness that comes from the gospel of peace. In addition to all this, take up the shield of faith, with which you can extinguish all the flaming arrows of the evil one. Take the helmet of salvation and the sword of the Spirit, which is the word of God. And pray in the Spirit on all occasions with all kinds of prayers and requests. With this in mind, be alert and always keep on praying for all the Lord's people. Pray also for me, that whenever I speak,

words may be given me so that I will fearlessly
make known the mystery of the gospel, for which
I am an ambassador in chains. Pray that I may
declare it fearlessly, as I should."

Ephesians 6:10-20, NIV

I fight writing these things down. I shake my
head. But I know I am called to walk forth with this truth
on my lips. I am called to share the truth. And I shake
my head slowly. No, Lord. Please someone else. Yet. I am
called for such a time as this.

"When I saw their fear, I stood and said to the
nobles, the officials, and the rest of the people:
'Do not be afraid of them; remember the Lord
who is great and awesome, and fight for your
brothers, your sons, your daughters, your wives,
and your houses.'"

Nehemiah 4:14, AMP

I am called to share why I feel this way. I
hated myself for a very long time. I sinned and was
unforgivable. But that's what Jesus came for. My
unforgivable sin. Because only He could take that sin

away. There is nothing on this earth that I can do to take it away. I know how I felt. How I feel today. I know the road I walked. I know the pain I felt. The sorrow I walked through. The part I played. The opportunity to say "no." But I didn't. Because I didn't want to give up what I had at that moment. It wasn't fair to my unborn child. It wasn't fair, really, to the world. Who knows what kind of leader he or she would have been born to be? Only God knows.

To those who say, "It's my body," I say, "That was used to create another, whether intentionally or not, your body was used to create another." You do not know who that body has been created to be. Or what world problems that baby was created to solve.

But to shift my thinking, my mindset more toward who I am today, which is positive, forgiving, and grateful. Blessed, having been shown mercy and grace. I have to say, nothing is beyond redemption. Unless you choose to be beyond redemption.

I give all the turmoil and trouble of these days to the Lord. We are called to share who God is. To share His goodness and mercy. To offer grace.

However, for those who choose not to accept that, we cannot force anyone. As the saying goes, you can lead a horse to water, but you cannot make him drink it. You can lead someone to salvation. But you cannot make them accept it.

Even Paul was a murderer. But he was not beyond redemption. Once he met Jesus and realized the truth, he became an avid follower. He lived, breathed, accepted chains, prison, and died for Jesus. He taught what he learned with passion. There's irony in me even saying that as I have been heard to say, "Not Paul again. He's so annoying!"

Mostly because he seemingly speaks against different groups at different times (i.e., women, slaves, children). However, I do think we need to look at his words in the context of the times and what was happening in that city, town, or village that he was speaking to.

I cannot imagine what Paul's thoughts would be about abortion. I would be curious to hear his thoughts on the subject. I have no doubt he would have prayed and then expressed his opinion.

OCTOBER 6, 2022

We all have choices to make with our lives—we choose what to wear, what to eat, where to live, sometimes where to work. But we also get to choose who or what we will worship. I cannot forget all that God has done for me. What He has brought me through, brought me out of. I will worship the Lord, and I will be content with all that I have and all that I am. He has strengthened me through hardship, through "easy" times, through struggles of my own making. I will worship the Lord always. He is faithful and He is a good, good God.

"But godliness with contentment is great gain."

1 Timothy 6:16, TPT

"Now fear the Lord and serve Him with all faithfulness. Throw away the gods your forefathers worshipped beyond the river and in Egypt, and serve the Lord. But if serving the Lord seems undesirable to you, then choose for yourselves this day whom you will serve, whether the gods your forefathers served beyond the river, or the gods of the Amorites, in whose land you are living. But as for me and my household, we will serve the Lord."

Joshua 24:14-15, TPT

OCTOBER 11, 2022

We all face trials. We won't know ahead of time what those trials are. But we are to consider it "joy." This Amplified version helps me understand better why the joy – "Be assured that the testing of your faith [through experience] produces endurance [leading to spiritual maturity, and inner peace]." That word "endurance" is one I can relate to. In order to make it to the end of a race, you have to continually train so that you have the endurance to last the distance of a race.

> "Consider it pure joy, my brethren, whenever you face trials of many kinds, because you know that the testing of your faith develops perseverance."

> James [Jacob] 1:2-3, TPT

> "The integrity of the upright guides them, but the unfaithful are destroyed by their duplicity."

> Proverbs 11:3, TPT

JUNE 5, 2023

Clearly, my past continued to haunt me. Over a year later and I still haven't done what He's called me to do. Share my journey. Share the pain. Share the redemption.

I've been thinking about choices. Ones we make, but also choices that people make under the guise of "I'm not hurting anyone." But really, aren't you? Isn't it possible that someone else can be hurt by your choices? I think it is.

My mom chose to go back to work that day. Even though she had, only hours earlier, finished working a double shift. I'll be honest, I can remember thinking how exhausted she looked. I chose not to say anything about that. She chose to go to work.

My dad chose to drive my mom to work. We'd had a heavy snowstorm, and he wanted to get her there safely. He also chose to pass a snowplow.

One by one, all those "choices" don't affect anyone else, right? Except, they didn't play individually. They collided with each other.

And the ripple is felt even today. Grandkids that barely remember their grandparents. Grandkids that never even had the opportunity to know them. Their kids' spouses who never had the pleasure of knowing them. And their grandkids' spouses that they never met. Or the generations that they might have still been alive, except for the choices made that day.

Some choices result in life, some result in death. Some result in self-judgment … that may last for decades. At times, our choices can result in anger at God.

Far too often, it takes too long to process that. We blame God for the choices that people make. We blame God (at least I have) for the choices I have made, which is ironic because really the only "thing" God did was give us free will, which means He gifted us with the ability to choose.

JULY 3, 2023

I missed my chance to share openly with all three of my children at one time about my abortion journey. I'm at a loss what to say, yet I do know. I want to tell them that, while it may sound so easy to have an abortion, it's the hardest thing I've ever done.

And yet, talking about it is hard too. That will forever be my life's greatest regret. Choosing to kill my child. I don't think they realize that they, too, carry a part of that sibling that they'll not know this side of heaven. Yes, I've felt shame, but regret is worse. Hating myself. Judging myself. I did not want to do it. But I felt like I had been backed into a corner.

I didn't think my parents would understand or support me. Looking back, I think I was wrong. Would they be upset? Probably, but I think, especially my mom, would have accepted my child. Would have loved her grandchild. My dad, too, but I think he would have been more of a challenge to get there. Still, he would have gotten there.

So yeah. My kids will never understand how I feel. I'm not even sure if they'll understand. But people need to know and understand that having an abortion can wreck someone. And if it doesn't, then I'm not sure they value human life. Yes, that's judgy. I'm letting that stand though. God values that life. No matter how that life is conceived. God values life. God will use lives to do great things, no matter the way of conception.

We have strayed so far from Him that we devalue so many things. Children, life, who He is.

SEPTEMBER 8, 2023

Lord, I do. My heart, my soul, my body crave You, Lord. I want more of You. I want to be with You; I want to know You more deeply. I want to go where You lead me. I want to have in my life all that You intend for me, to trust You more completely. My heart, my being wants to receive and accept all that You have for me. I love You so much, Lord. I'm so thankful You are my God! Amen and Hallelujah!

"As the deer longs for streams of water,
so I long for you, O God.
I thirst for God, the living God.
When can I go and stand before him?"

Psalm 42:1-2, TPT

SEPTEMBER 16, 2023

Lord, my heart desires you alone. Help me remember to leave the doors shut that you have closed. Doors of shame, frustration, unforgiveness. Remind me that I now live life as a dreamer, forgiving and FORGIVEN child of YOURS—I am yours, Lord. Thank You for Your grace to keep me from thinking less of myself than You think of me. Thank You for the people who shine the light on Your path that remind me of whose I am, of the good, good child You have created me to be. Thank You for the gifts of compassion, encouragement, and humor. Thank You for the gifts that I am still dreaming of and unlocking, that I have not fully believed in yet. Open my eyes, Lord, to all You've created me to be. Open my heart so that You can pour light and love into me and so that You can lavish all Your love—that I accept and go forth sharing that light and love with others. I can't give more than what I've accepted from You, Lord. I accept You, and I love You, Lord. My heart is filled with You, Lord— let my works and actions only show You, Lord, how beautiful and amazing You are. How great You are, God. Thank You, Lord, for life itself. I love You, Lord! Amen.

"In his kindness God called you to share in his eternal glory by means of Christ Jesus. So after you have suffered a little while, he will restore, support, and strengthen you, and he will place you on a firm foundation."

1 Peter 5:10, TPT

OCTOBER 23, 2023

Me again. Yes, God is still prompting me. Prompting me to go back to come forward again. I made a terrible choice. One I felt I had to make.

My childhood, as far as childhoods go, was actually pretty good. I was fed, cared for, loved. There are only a few times that I can remember things I'd rather forget. Many people had that uncle. You know the one. "Oh, go ahead and sit on his lap, it's not a big deal." But I really didn't want to. As far as I remember, he didn't "do" anything, but I just didn't want to. Still, I had to.

The birthday spanking when I was five-ish … over my dad's knee. I hit my nose on the wall and was told it was my fault because I was squirming. Seriously, what five year old wants to be spanked, even in "fun"?

The night my dad and the doctor friend of my mom's decided a political conversation would be the "fun" topic. The problem for me was that, when they started talking, they also started drinking. And they would get loud. Because it didn't matter what they actually believed, one would pick one side, the other would pick the other side, and they would "debate." But not what we think of as a debate. It was loud. It would go late into the night. As a child, it was impossible to fall asleep. Yelling and shouting. Of course, there was cursing. It was so unnerving for me, as a child. Of course, I whined about it. We were at their house, so the response was simply ... "Shut up and go lay back down on the sofa."

What I heard and carried with me for decades was that my voice didn't matter. I didn't connect that until I was sixty-something. It's never too late to learn, but still. Yes, sometimes I wish I had known that my voice mattered.

In my seventh grade art class, I was told I was stupid. Drawing wasn't my strength. It still isn't, but I can draw! Looking back, I realize the only thing stupid was that man's comment. He taught me to compare myself to others. Again, this was something I would need to unlearn and replace with something else.

During my seventh-grade year, I had taken Conversational Spanish with the goal of continuing on through high school. The seventh grade was split in half. Half took Spanish, and the other half took French. We were supposed to roll up into the same subject in eighth grade. Guess what happened. Yep, you guessed it. The entire class had their schedules flipped, and everyone who took Spanish was assigned French. Those who took French were assigned Spanish.

I didn't want to take French, but "they" said nothing could be done. I wanted my parents to go to the school, but for whatever reason, my schedule didn't change back to Spanish. A small handful of kids were able to get their schedules changed. Mind you, I do feel that today, there are too many times when parents rush in to "fix" things for their kids, but I do think sometimes it's justified. Still today, I wish I had been listened to.

Not all my memories are negative. I was athletic. I loved basketball and softball, and I was decent at both. I had many trophies from those days. We did travel a fair amount as a family. I saw a good bit of the USA while growing up. We camped; my dad retrofitted a van into a camping van.

NOVEMBER 11, 2023

Lord, that spirit of offense in me. Root it out. Help me to see it when it shows up, help me to recognize it and replace that with patience, mercy, and forgiveness. Help me to move beyond. Help me to understand where it comes from so that through You, I can overcome it. I want to give the glory to You, Lord. Thank you, Holy Spirit, for the peace You bring me, the conviction in my life where I need it, and the gentle nudging and loving You give me. I love You so much, Lord. Amen.

"Good sense makes one slow to anger,
and it is his glory to overlook an offense."

Proverbs 19:11, TPT

NOVEMBER 20, 2023

Lord, thank You, thank You, thank You! Thank You for showing me who You are—Love—not as I've always thought of love, but as what love truly is. You are faithful, compassionate, good, generous; You remember Your promises. Even when I falter, You remember and will fulfill those promises. You are merciful and full of grace. You offer grace and mercy—all the time. Help me to show that same grace and mercy. Help me to leave offense behind me and only reflect Your love as best I can or better only in a supernatural way—because that's how You do all things … supernaturally! Help me show Your love, God. Help me remember that like Joseph and so many before me, You are refining me and that Your blessings are just around the next corner. May I never stop seeking You and the blessings You have for me. I love You, Lord! Amen.

"Know therefore that the Lord your God is
God, the faithful God who keeps covenant and
steadfast love with those who love
him and keep his commandments, to a
thousand generations..."

Deuteronomy 7:9,
English Standard Version (ESV)

NOVEMBER 22, 2023

Lord, help me remember that, where I am and what I've experienced will be used by You for good to help others. Help me keep my vision on what I can, no, on what You can do for others through me. I pray I am always open for ways that You can use me—to help others see who You really are—a kind, loving God who desires a relationship with your creation. I praise You, Lord, and thank You for all You do. Right now, I am thankful for the gift of time, even when I abuse that gift. You bless me in spite of myself. In spite of me wanting to waste time in bed! You still bless me. Thank You, Father. I love You. Amen.

"And now do not be distressed or angry with yourselves because you sold me here, for God sent me before you to preserve life."

Genesis 45:5, TPT

DECEMBER 1, 2023

Beloved Father, thank You for adopting me so that I may call You that. Abba, Daddy, Father. You are love, You are beloved, You are Father. May I walk out my life knowing I am more than enough because I am Yours. Help me respond to Your nudges and stop living in fear. Today, fear is no more! I love You, Abba! Amen.

"So you have not received a spirit that makes you fearful slaves. Instead, you received God's Spirit when he adopted you as his own children. Now we call him, 'Abba, Father.'"

Romans 8:15, NLT

DECEMBER 7, 2023

Father, thank You for shedding light on things that I fear, things that make me lukewarm in my faith. Although I am still struggling with being vocal, help that fear not control me. Help me to use the voice and experiences You've given me to shine a bright light on You and to Your love and forgiveness. I've become so entrenched in being satisfied and complacent. Help me be bold—show me where You need to be magnified. Show me where Your love needs to shine and give me the words to shine Your light! I love You so much,
Abba. Amen.

> "So, because you are lukewarm, and neither hot nor cold, I will spit you out of my mouth."

> Revelation 3:16, ESV

DECEMBER 13, 2023

Father, thank You for this journey. Thank You for choosing me. Help me be that instrument to show others the utter joy of knowing You—trusting You, believing in You, believing in Your redemption, forgiveness, life! Help me shout from the rooftops the night and day difference You make in my life! I love You, Lord—forever!! Amen!

> "But you are not like that, for you are a chosen people. You are royal priests, a holy nation, God's very own possession. As a result, you can show others the goodness of God, for he called you out of the darkness into his wonderful light."

1 Peter 2:9-10, NLT

Father, thank You for clarity, for the reminder to worship You and You alone. Thank You for the testimony you have given me. For the testimony of Jesus. Thank You that a testimony is a way of prophesy, if You did it once, You can and will do it again. There are others who need healing Lord—in so many ways. Help me share my testimony that they may (1) see You! and (2) see that healing is not only possible, but will happen with You as the guide and great healer! I love how You work, God, and I love how You work in me, and I just LOVE YOU! Amen!

"Then I fell down at his feet to worship him, but he said, 'No, don't worship me. I am a servant of God, just like you and your brothers and sisters who testify about their faith in Jesus. Worship only God. For the essence of prophecy is to give a clear witness for Jesus.'"

Revelation 19:10, NLT

DECEMBER 22, 2023

What a gift to read this entire passage and exchange the word "love" with "Jesus" every time! The clarity of my need for Jesus, the understanding that without Jesus, I don't have anything—for sure I don't have love! And why? Because YOU ARE LOVE! Without you, all three, the trinity, we cannot truly know love. Not in the way you intended love to be displayed. Holy, giving, unselfish. Help me show that love to others. Help me show others Christ in me. Show me who needs to see You, show me the path to walk and give me the words to be truth in light. That You are known as light and that others want a relationship with You as You want with them. I love You. Thank You for Jesus being in my heart! Amen.

Jesus is patient and kind. Jesus is not jealous or boastful or proud or rude. He does not demand his own way. He is not irritable, and he keeps no record of being wronged. He does not rejoice about injustice but rejoices whenever the truth wins out. Jesus never gives up, never loses faith, is always hopeful, and endures through every circumstance.

Prophecy and speaking in unknown languages and special knowledge will become useless. But Jesus will last forever! Now our knowledge is partial and incomplete, and even the gift of prophecy reveals only part of the whole picture! But when the time of perfection comes, these partial things will become useless.

"When I was a child, I spoke and thought
and reasoned as a child. But when I grew up,
I put away childish things. Now we see things
imperfectly, like puzzling reflections in a mirror,
but then we will see everything with perfect
clarity. All that I know now is partial and
incomplete, but then I will know everything
completely, just as God now knows
me completely.

Three things will last forever—faith, hope, and Jesus—and the greatest of these is Jesus."

1 Corinthians 13:4-13, NLT

JANUARY 17 AND 18, 2024

Purpose—sharing God's redemptive message. What hope and glory to God is found here in Joshua! God, I have put You in a box so neatly and tightly wrapped. Help me grow in understanding all of You—Father, Son, and Holy Spirit! Not that I will ever know all of You but give me greater understanding! I love You so much and am so grateful for Your redemption! Amen.

ADDENDUM

I know my identity and purpose starts with knowing You, Father. You are Redeemer, Forgiver. You are Love. You are Strong. You are wise and understanding. You are Guide. You are Present (in EVERY sense of that word!). You are glorious and bold and TRUTH and honesty and joy and peace. You are EVERYTHING! You are CREATOR! Amen!

> "Be strong and courageous! For the Lord your
> God is with you wherever you go."

Joshua 1:9, NLT

FEBRUARY 7, 2024

Thank You, God, for being with me always. For holding me and loving me in every area of my life. Help me see how much You love me every day of my life—in all the situations of my life. I love You so much and want to get to know You deeper every day! Amen!

"For the Lord your God is living among you.
He is a mighty savior.
He will take delight in you with gladness.
With his love, he will calm all your fears.
He will rejoice over you with joyful songs."

Zephaniah 3:17, NLT

MARCH 13 AND 17, 2024

Father, I am cranky today. I've been cranky. Help me release that ugly. What is on my mind that I act this way? Thank You for Holy Spirit, to come and free me from the demons. I praise You, O God! Fill my mind with thoughts of You, with worship for You!
My heart is Yours, Lord. Mold me and shape me in Your image. Adjust my attitude when I'm not mirroring You. I want no evil to be in my heart at all—only You, Lord. I love You so much!

"So humble yourselves before God. Resist the devil, and he will flee from you."

James 4:7, NLT

APRIL 2, 2024

Note: The reading for that day was Matthew 11:7-11. I may have read that, but the verse at the bottom of my journal is what I needed.

Although I write this on April 3, I love the Psalm 46:10 below because on April 2, I needed time with You. I needed to stop and listen. This is true every day. I need You, Lord. Help me remember that. Always. I love You.

"Be still, and know that I am God!"

Psalm 46:10, NKJV

MAY 19, 2024

To know You, God, is to experience You. Like I did when my parents died, and I knew You were holding me. In all our moves, You've been with us. In my joy, in my sorrow, You are the constant! I want to experience more of You every day! I love You!

"The joy of the Lord is your strength!"

Nehemiah 8:10, NKJV

JUNE 24, 2024

Use me, Father. I may not "feel" ready, but truly if we go by how I feel, will I ever "feel" ready? I'm laying down and surrendering to You. I trust You to mold me into who You purpose me to be. Only may I walk in obedience and become the person You are calling me to be. I love You more every day.

"Loving God means keeping his commandments,
and his commandments are
not burdensome."

1 John 5:3, NLT

AUGUST 6, 2024

Thank You, Lord, for the reminder today that I am to tell the story of who You are. I am to share all the ways and glorious things You have done for me. That I am to praise You for doing the same for all generations and everyone whose life You touched—EVERYONE—they need only to look and see You. I will write them down so those stories/testimonies are there to see where You are in my life—always! Even the times I falter—you are there to pick me up and help me walk forward again. Every time! You are so faithful! I love You so much, God!

"Let each generation tell its children of your mighty acts; let them proclaim your power."

Psalm 145:4, NLT

AUGUST 23, 2024

Lord, we say clarity is kindness today. For me that means doing what You're calling me to do—use my voice to shine a light toward you and against child trafficking and to write my book … our book. Help me remember it's Your voice I'm following—not my own. That it's Your calling—not my opinions. I love to pursue You, Father. I love to seek Your will, and I will follow You everywhere! I want more of You, Lord—I will finish this race. I will never quit! I love You! Again, with Joshua 1:9 in my journal: "Be strong and courageous! For the Lord your God is with you whereever you go." Amen!

"I have fought the good fight, I have finished the race, and I have remained faithful."

1 Timothy 4:7, NIV

SEPTEMBER 30, 2024

Choosing trust. Choosing Your word. Choosing belief. Hiding in the secret place of Your presence. Safe. You are my rock, Lord. A firm foundation. The place and the one I can go to and seek You for truth, light, life. You are love—no one can know love except by You. Transform and renew my mind—daily—sometimes by minutes! To walk in Your will—whole and complete. To walk in Your purpose for me. Using my voice so that Your truth may be known. I love You!

"Don't copy the behavior and customs of this world, but let God transform you into a new person by changing the way you think. Then you will learn to know God's will for you, which is good and pleasing and perfect."

Romans 12:2, NLT

OCTOBER 23, 2024

What am I thinking today? What are my emotions today?

I'm tired, sad, downtrodden. Feeling like a failure. Feeling like I must not trust God if I'm not writing a book He has called me to write. I'm thinking that perhaps I'm unfaithful and disobedient. My head hurts, my stomach has been hurting—in the past I've had that when I'm being disobedient. I'm afraid to re-read what I've already written. Will it cause pain? Will it make sense? Will it be interesting? Today is a struggle. I don't feel good about myself or what I'm doing or not doing. I feel phony and like I'm playing a role. I feel like Elijah. Sometimes I win the biggest battles, and then I run in fear and I'm tired and don't want to go on! Sometimes I hate myself so much for what I've done, how I murdered my baby, that I treat my husband and kids erratically because I just refuse to let go of hating myself. How many times do I have to replay this in my mind? I have to stop hating myself. Out of my heart is really what I believe. God does not hate me. I have to stop hating me. God loves me. I love me. I am worthy of being loved by myself.

"My child, pay attention to what I say.
Listen carefully to my words.
Don't lose sight of them.
Let them penetrate deep into your heart,
for they bring life to those who find them,
and healing to their whole body."

Proverbs 4:20-22, NLT

NOVEMBER 19, 2024

Reading through journal entries from the years while writing this book has me thinking about how grateful I am that God never gave up on me. He's asked me time and time again to come and write this book. I left it and would find myself prompted and would come back. Through all of this, God was with me. Holy Spirit guiding and nudging me to write this down. Share your story. There's someone who needs to hear it.

I said earlier that this is not for everyone. Not everyone will agree with me. Some will be triggered; some will be angry. I understand that.

But this is for those who need to hear that God does indeed love you, despite what has happened in your life. For those who have done something they deem unforgivable. This is a reminder that Jesus died for you too. That God knew your life before you were formed. God loves you. God wants a relationship with you. He is calling you to come to Him.

You are forgiven. You are loved.

Come as you are, winter is over. Spring has come.

JANUARY 24, 2025

I had hoped to have my book finished and published by today. But I am again reminded of how redeeming God is and how much He loves me. I have cried out to Him to not actually write this, to not share this part of my life. But He loves me through that.

There are so many things I didn't want known about me, and that I have struggled to forgive myself for, that I thought others would not forgive me for. But the bottom line is that God has heard me. He has forgiven me, a very long time ago. He forgave me before I was born. With each word I write, with each plea I make, I am forgiven. He has mercy on me. He offers me grace. He redeems me. From everything, I am redeemed. As are you.

"Out of the depths I have cried to You, O Lord;
Lord, hear my voice! Let Your ears be attentive
To the voice of my supplications. If You, Lord,
should mark iniquities, O Lord, who could stand?
But there is forgiveness with You, That You may
be feared. I wait for the Lord, my soul waits, And
in His word I do hope. My soul waits for the Lord
More than those who watch for the morning—
Yes, more than those who watch for the morning.
O Israel, hope in the Lord; For with the Lord
there is mercy, And with Him is abundant
redemption. And He shall redeem Israel From all
his iniquities."

Psalms 130:1-8, NKJV

FEBRUARY 3, 2025

The redemption. I read Psalm 139 this morning. My initial focus was on the verses near the end. The ones that focused on others' sins and how they were against God. And the reminder that I, too, have sinned against God. But then as I was looking at the footnotes, verse 16 caught my eye. Again, my tears flow.

But it was different today. Today it wasn't in self-condemnation or self-hatred. But just because I was sad. Sad that on this side of heaven I won't see the purpose God had for him. Sad that he didn't have a chance. But I know that I am forgiven. By God, by my son, even by myself.

You know, in a way redemption is a choice too. You can reject redemption. You can keep living in rejection. I do not recommend that. The peace of accepting redemption is so much more beautiful.

He knew my book. He loved me despite it. He redeemed me because of it. He loves me right through it.

I'm grateful forever to God. To Jesus. To Holy Spirit. Each has had a role. God called me to write. Jesus forgave and redeemed me. Holy Spirit has comforted me, led me, and guided me through this journey. My heart is His.

> "You saw me before I was born. Every day of my life was recorded in your book. Every moment was laid out before a single day had passed."
>
> Psalms 139:16, NLT

ACKNOWLEDGMENTS

To my husband, Joey, thank you for allowing me the space in my heart and life to write and finish this book. Even on those rainy days when my moods and feelings were as gray as the sky was, or as stormy as the day may have been. I appreciate you listening as I processed. I love you with all my heart!

To my children and their families, Little Timmy; Angela, Collin, Austin and Mason; Julie; Zack and Shae, your permission and acceptance of me helped me move forward in ways you may never understand. Your support helped me when I wanted to quit, whether you're aware of that or not.

To Sandy and Cary Moorman, thank you for being the first light of Jesus in my life through my parents departing. For teaching me who Jesus really is, even though it's taken me years of my own Jesus Journey to really gain a deeper understanding. It's a journey I won't be leaving anytime soon.

To my Cheerleader Friends – Amy, Marlisa, and Jessica. You have all been a sounding board and such great support to me. You've given me so much encouragement, joy, challenge, and laughter. Let's explore a bit more about the mosquito, shall we?

To my Book Club friends – Jill, Sheryl, and April. Thank you for the decades we've shared life as we poured over the stories in the lives of the characters of the books we've read. We've also shared so much of life. I'm sorry I never told you about this part of my life, but I believe you will understand.

To Brooke Kanitz, for being the first coach to encourage me to begin journaling how I felt and to encourage, yet again to seek His forgiveness. And to Dr. Tina Hay for being the second coach to encourage me to actually write this book and help me detox my soul. To all the pastors over the years that have counseled me through unforgiveness. Although I continued to come back to other pastors to seek forgiveness, each step was a step forward in that journey.

To Jacquie McIver, for so much advice and guidance while working through editing and finishing my book. Your help has been immense and so appreciated.

To Windy Goodloe, for being a patient editor, teaching me how to do editing and asking questions and helping me flush out my thoughts!

To Courtney Monday, no book is complete without a fantastic design and illustration. You heard my thoughts even though I had no idea what I was looking for and created exactly what I wanted. I'm beyond thankful for the touches you've added to make this all that I dreamed it would be!

There are so many more people throughout my life that I appreciate helping me. God has placed you all in my life, sometimes for a season, but all for a reason. You have blessed me!

May God bless each and every one of you tenfold how you've blessed me!

My prayer for each of you that contributed to or read this book:

"Now Jabez called on the God of Israel, saying, 'Oh that You would greatly bless me and extend my border, and that Your hand might be with me, and that You would keep me from harm so that it would not hurt me!' And God brought about what he requested."

1 Chronicles 4:10, NIV

ABOUT THE AUTHOR

Kathy Tomlinson is a wife of thirty-four years, a mom, and a proud "Omie" who believes in second chances, slow mornings, the unconditional love of dogs, and the healing power of fresh air. She's an author and health coach with a heart for honest conversations, messy stories, and the quiet strength it takes to start over.

Through her own seasons of heartbreak, hard choices, and unexpected redemption, she's learned that healing doesn't come all at once—and it rarely looks the way we imagined. She's learned that, sometimes, picking up the pieces is the bravest thing you can do.

When she's not writing or coaching, you'll likely find her walking under open skies or enjoying her dogs.

After Winter Comes Spring is her invitation to walk with you through the cold places—and into the quiet hope of something new.

www.ingramcontent.com/pod-product-compliance
Lightning Source LLC
Chambersburg PA
CBHW070328130626
46556CB00007B/2772